PLAYS OF THE YEAR

Volume 48

'I do not claim that they are the best plays of their period. I submit merely that all are good of their kind, and that they share qualities for which a true playgoer looks.'

Preface to *Plays of the Year*, Volume One, 1949

PLAYS OF THE YEAR

EDITED BY
J. C. TREWIN

LARK RISE
Keith Dewhurst from the
book by Flora Thompson

MEMOIR
John Murrell

BODIES
James Saunders

VOLUME 48

PAUL ELEK
GRANADA PUBLISHING
London Toronto Sydney New York

GRANADA PUBLISHING LIMITED
Frogmore, St Albans, Herts AL2 2NF
and
3 Upper James Street, London W1R 4BP
Suite 405, 4th Floor, 866 United Nations Plaza, New York,
NY 10017, USA
117 York Street, Sydney, NSW 2000, Australia
100 Skyway Avenue, Rexdale, Ontario M9W 3A6, Canada
PO Box 84165, Greenside, 2034 Johannesburg, South Africa
61 Beach Road, Auckland, New Zealand

Published by Granada Publishing *in* Paul Elek Ltd 1980

ISBN 0 236 40168 8

Printed in Great Britain by
Clarke, Doble & Brendon Ltd.
Plymouth

FOR WENDY
Remembering Guelph

CONTENTS

INTRODUCTION

' 'Tis a country diversion,' drawls Millamant in
The Way of the World. 'I loathe the country and
everything that relates to it.' In the circumstances,
the dear woman might not have enjoyed LARK
RISE, Keith Dewhurst's dramatised version of
Flora Thompson's book, which is the most
enchanting rural play of our time (and also the
first National Theatre production to appear in this
series).

The English theatre, unlike the Irish, has been
short of true rustic plays. So many have been in
the Cold Comfort manner without the light in
Stella Gibbons's eye; scenes from the kind of
country that Sydney Smith — who would be in
tune with Millamant — called a healthy grave
where he feared creation might expire before
tea-time. Otherwise, the stage has been occupied
too often by a curious assortment of local yokels,
the town condescending (as it never should) to the
country. Nowadays we seldom speak of the
Devonian Eden Phillpotts, but he did know how
to write folk-comedy with an aphoristic wisdom
that acted as a preservative.

LARK RISE, quite another matter again, is
based principally on the first volume of Flora
Thompson's trilogy, Lark Rise to Candleford. She
was born in 1876, as Flora Jane Timms, in the
Oxfordshire hamlet of Juniper Hill: her mother
had been a nursemaid in a good family and her
father was a stonemason (the more envious said a
bricklayer). Ultimately, Flora became a postmistress,

married John Thompson who was a post-office clerk, and lived in Bournemouth where she wrote the childhood sketches that one day would develop into a trilogy: Lark Rise *(1939),* Over to Candleford *(1941), and* Candleford Green *(1943). She died at Brixham, Devon, in 1948.*

As Keith Dewhurst has miraculously compressed it for the theatre, LARK RISE is a true pastoral, wholly honest, with never a hint of synthetic Wurzel-in-the-Wold invention. The dramatist has contrived to fit the principal events of the book into a single day. Though it may be argued that the hamlet was hardly so busy a place as this, it is as absorbing in the text as in the theatre to observe the to-and-fro under a wide sky that changes from the glow of daybreak over the wheatfields to the star-strewn canopy of a calm country night. Bees swarm; the mowers, their scythes laid by, relax in their dinner break; travelling shopmen bring their goods to Lark Rise; the postman arrives, knowing the secret of everything he carries (as he did in my own village in the far South-West); a soldier is home from the Sudan; a local chatterer pays her call ('standing gossips always stay longest'); and a 12-year-old girl contemplates service in what was known as a 'petty place'. ('Garibaldi' stands for the potential mistress, who wears a Garibaldi jacket):

GARIBALDI: Can you do what you're told?

MARTHA: Yes, mum.

GARIBALDI: Well that sounds right. This isn't a hard place because although there are sixteen rooms only three or four of them are in use. Can you get up at six without being called?

MARTHA: Yes, mum.

GARIBALDI: There's the kitchen range to light

INTRODUCTION 9

and the flues to be swept once a week, the
dining-room to be swept and dusted and the
fire lit before breakfast. I'm down myself in
time to prepare breakfast. No cooking's
required, beyond preparing vegetables.
MARTHA: Yes, mum.
GARIBALDI: After breakfast you'll help me
with the beds and turning out the rooms and
paring the potatoes and so on; and after
dinner there's plenty to do — washing-up,
cleaning knives and boots and polishing silver.
MARTHA: Yes, mum.
GARIBALDI: There'll be more jobs in the
evening of course, but at nine o'clock you'll
be free to go to bed — after placing hot water
in my bedroom.
MARTHA: Yes, mum.
GARIBALDI: Then, as wages, I can offer you
two pounds ten a year. It is not a great wage
but you are very small and you'll have an easy
place and a comfortable home. You won't feel
lonely, will you?
MARTHA: No, mum.
GARIBALDI: Tell your mother I shall expect
her to fit you out well. You will want caps and
aprons. I like my maids to look neat. And tell
her to let you bring plenty of changes, for we
only wash once in six weeks. I have a woman
to do it all up.
MARTHA: Yes, mum.
GARIBALDI: Well I shall expect you next
Monday then.
MARTHA: Yes, mum . . .

But she did not take the job.
Though narrative is secondary in LARK RISE,
we get to know the villagers as intimates: the
young schoolgirl, Laura — who is Flora Thompson

herself — her parents up at the end cottage (which in Juniper Hill today is called Lark Rise Cottage), the labourers and women of the village, the travelling tradesmen and local eccentrics, the children, the bailiff, the squire, the innkeeper — at late evening we are in the hamlet taproom — an entire community in the movement of a long summer day.

That, in its own fashion, was the method of Under Milk Wood, *but LARK RISE is neither so single-minded nor so idiosyncratic. It is marvellously of its period, never sentimentally idyllic, though its harsher events — such as the sending of an old man to the workhouse — are not accentuated unwisely. This is a record of what was even then a swiftly disappearing rural England exemplified by life 'on a gentle rise in the flat, wheat-growing north-east corner of Oxfordshire.' Flora Thompson went on: 'We will call it Lark Rise because of the great number of skylarks which made the surrounding fields their springboard and nested on the bare earth between the rows of green corn.'*

In the Cottesloe auditorium of the National, Bill Bryden and Sebastian Graham-Jones put on LARK RISE as a 'promenade' production. This means, roughly, that audience and players were intermingled; that you could be swept along with the company and have a brisk evening ensuring, at this place or the other, that you were still in touch with the action. Ingenious and enjoyable; but, personally, I was happy to find a seat on an upper tier and look down on both players and surging audience: from the first mushrooming to that affecting coda, the church service and a sudden imaginative flash forward, across the years, to the reading of a casualty-roll after the first world war.

II

MEMOIR, by the expert Canadian dramatist, John Murrell, returns to us probably the most legendary of all actresses, Sarah Bernhardt (1844-1923). I met the play first in Guelph, Ontario, where Professor Eric Salmon, Chairman of the Department of Drama in the University of Guelph, had organised a conference on the international stage in the Bernhardt era. Many of the major players from eighty or so years ago seemed to haunt the conference rooms during addresses by more than twenty scholars from Canada, the United States, France, and Britain; close by were performances of Mr Murrell's play in which Bernhardt, at Belle-Isle off the Breton coast, and in the twilight of her career — she had only twelve months to live — was involved with a second autobiographical book. In the words of Professor Salmon, who directed: 'The purpose of the play is imaginative, not documentary . . . its real focus being on the capacity of art to make life immortal; or, conversely, the capacity of life to embrace and retain something of the immortal gesture of art. The title gives the right clue: this is not a play about Sarah Bernhardt; it is a play about art and the artist. But Bernhardt is a marvellous touchstone for these themes.'

She is indeed: the piece — with actress and secretary discussing an imaginary second volume — is an uncanny creative feat, as London realised when the two-character play reached the Ambassadors Theatre in January 1978, Siobhán McKenna still in temperamental blaze. Bernhardt, even at twilight, was the woman of whom Stephen Phillips had written lushly when in 1912 she came to the Coliseum, of all theatres:

Now panther stealing on its prey,

Now waking lark in breaking day,
Now tigress crouching in her lair,
Then dove afloat in summer air,
Enchantress of the voice of gold . . .

and so on.

Yes, dreadful; but most people who tried to write about Bernhardt went astray. She was indescribable. Possibly Maurice Baring put it best when he called her 'one of the permanent and beautiful guesses of mankind.' Mr Murrell's play, with its wider implications, is an inspired guess.

III

Hampstead Theatre had another uncommon success in a long sequence when it staged BODIES by a wise and versatile dramatist, James Saunders, author — among much else — of Next Time I'll Sing to You *and* A Scent of Flowers.

The play must speak for itself. Briefly, it is an attack on a world of materialism, one without faith, one that denies the existence of anything we can neither touch nor see. At first it looks like being a sophisticated quartet-comedy. Two couples meet after long separation; once, it seems, for a short time they had exchanged partners; we wonder whether there will be another shift. By no means. The duller of the couples, back from America, have been converted there by a form of comfortable therapy that shuts out things of the spirit; they have become, in fact, dangerously dreary. In the second half the play resolves itself into a post-prandial battle in which a headmaster argues with eloquence against the kind of 'coming to terms' that excludes art, poetry, intimations of immortality. His emotion is heightened by the tragedy of a sensitive schoolboy, something that is simply reported to us and supplies a final curtain.

What matters is the fury of his teacher's attack on the material view, the deadening of the spirit.

J. C. TREWIN

Hampstead, 1980.

I am most grateful to my colleague, Sandra Gorman, for her patient and understanding help.

NOTE

Bodies, in Volume 48, is the tenth Hampstead Theatre production included in **Plays of the Year**. The previous choices have been:

LARK RISE

by
Keith Dewhurst

from the book by
Flora Thompson

LARK RISE

Lark Rise opened at the Cottesloe (National Theatre) on 29 March 1978, with the following cast:

LAURA	*Caroline Embling*
EDMUND	*Laurence Hardiman*
EMMA TIMMS	*Mary Miller*
ALBERT TIMMS	*James Grant*
BISHIE/POSTIE	*Trevor Ray*
BOAMER/CHEAPJACK	*Warren Clarke*
PUMPKIN/DOCTOR/SQUIRE BRACEWELL	
	Derek Newark
OLD PRICE/DICK/GRANDFATHER	*John Barrett*
OLD DAVID/MAJOR SHARMAN/RECTOR	
	Michael Gough
MR MORRIS/JERRY PARISH/	
LANDLORD	*Brian Glover*
FISHER/JOHN PRICE/CARRIER	*Glyn Grain*
STUT/TWISTER/ALGY/TRAMP	*Howard Goorney*
MRS SPICER/OLD SALLY/MRS MILLER/	
MRS ANDREWS	*June Watson*
MRS BLABY/MRS BEAMISH/GARIBALDI JACKET	
	Dinah Stabb
MRS PEVERILL/QUEENIE MACEY	*Edna Doré*
MR PRIDHAM/SAM/SINGER	*Martin Carthy*
MARTHA BEAMISH/POLLY	*Louisa Livingstone*
COCKIE/SINGER	*John Tams*
SINGER	*Shirley Collins*

The Albion Band

Directed by Bill Bryden and
Sebastian Graham-Jones
Designed by William Dudley
Lighting by William Dudley and Laurence Clayton
Music directed by Ashley Hutchings

It was revived on 6 September, with the following variations in the cast:

LAURA	*Valerie Whittington*
EDMUND	*Paul Davies-Prowles*
ALBERT TIMMS	*Mark McManus*
	(at 12 performances)
BISHIE/POSTIE	*Peter Armitage*
	(at 7 performance)
BOAMER	*Jack Shepherd*
OLD DAVID/DICK	*Harry Lomax*
OLD PRICE/GRANDFATHER	*Bill Owen*
FISHER/JOHN PRICE	*Frederick Warder*
	(at 12 performances)
MRS BLABY/MRS BEAMISH/GARIBALDI	
JACKET	*Tamara Hinchco*
	(with Dinah Stabb at 10 performances)
MAJOR SHARMAN/RECTOR/CHEAPJACK	*Dave King*
MARTHA BEAMISH/POLLY	*Julia Brams*
	(at 12 performances)

Assistant to the Directors Celia Bannerman

And it was revived again on 28 March 1979, with the following variations in the cast:

PUMPKIN/RECTOR	*Mark McManus*
DOCTOR/SQUIRE	*Gawn Grainger*
MRS BLABY/MRS BEAMISH/GARIBALDI JACKET	
	Anna Carteret
DAVID/DICK/MAJOR SHARMAN	*J. G. Devlin*
CHEAPJACK	*Peter Armitage*

CHARACTERS

LAURA (10)

EDMUND (8)

EMMA TIMMS (Laura & Edmund's mother)

ALBERT TIMMS (Laura & Edmund's father)

BISHIE (Bill Miller)

BOAMER (Dick Tuffrey)

PUMPKIN (Tom Gaskin) } Farm labourers

OLD PRICE

DAVID (Boamer's father)

MR MORRIS (Bailiff — ''Old Monday Morning'')

FISHER (youth)

STUT

MRS SPICER (leader of the women's gang)

MRS BLABY

MRS PEVERILL

MRS MILLER

OLD SALLY (80)

DICK (her husband)

OLD POSTIE (the postman)

MR SHARMAN (the Major)

DOCTOR

CARRIER

GRANDFATHER (Emma's father)

QUEENIE MACEY

TWISTER (her husband)

JERRY PARISH (fish/fruit cart)

MARTHA BEAMISH (12)

MRS BEAMISH

SQUIRE BRACEWELL

JOHN PRICE (son of Old Price)

MRS ANDREWS

GARIBALDI JACKET

CHEAPJACK (tinker)

TRAMP

POLLY (Fisher's girl)

LANDLORD OF THE PUB

ALGY

MR PRIDHAM (Band singer)

RECTOR

SAM

COCKIE

ACT ONE

The band welcomes the audience into the space with a tune. When the lights go down the actors form up a photo pose, and as the lights come up again, the band singers begin

ARISE AND PICK A POSY

Hark says the fair maid
The nightingales are singing,
The larks they are winging
Their notes up in the air.
Small birds and turtle doves
On every bough are building,
The sun is just a-glimmering
 Arise my dear.

Rise up my fair one
And pick your love a posy,
It is the finest flower
That ever my eyes did see.
Yes I will pick you posies,
Sweet lily, pink and rosy;
There is none so fair a flower
As the lad I adore.

Lemady, Lemady
You are a lovely creature,
You are the finest flower
That ever my eyes did see.
I play you a tune
All on the pipes of ivory,
So early in the morning,
Before break of day.

Arise and pick a posy,
Sweet lily, pink and rosy;

It is the finest flower
That ever I did see.
Small birds and turtle doves
On every bough are building,
The sun is just a-glimmering
Arise my dear.

(The cast has now dispersed except for LAURA, who is a small, skinny girl of ten with dark eyes and pale yellow hair. She now speaks to the audience)

LAURA: The hamlet stood on a gentle rise in the flat, wheat-growing, north-east corner of Oxfordshire. We will call it Lark Rise because of the great number of skylarks which made the surrounding fields their springboard and nested on the bare earth between the rows of green corn. For a few days or a week or a fortnight, the fields stood 'ripe unto harvest'. It was the one perfect period in the hamlet year. The 'Eighties brought a succession of hot summers, and day after day, as harvest time approached, the children of the end house would wake to the dewy pearly pink of a fine summer dawn, and the swizzh, swizzh of the early morning breeze rustling through the ripe corn beyond their doorstep . . .

(LAURA's brother, EDMUND appears, yawning and rubbing his eyes. He is eight years old, and tall for his age, with blue eyes and regular features)

LAURA: Oh come on, Edmund. Come you on.
EDMUND: What are we goin' for?
LAURA: Mushrooms, Edmund.

(EDMUND is excited)

EDMUND: Mushrooms?!
LAURA: Sssh! Mushrooms!

*(LAURA and EDMUND lose themselves in the
wheatfield that is the audience. The light is the
pearly pink of dawn)*

Scene 1
MEN GOING TO WORK

*In the end house Laura's father ALBERT TIMMS
is eating a piece of bread and lard. He is a slim
upright man with fiery eyes and raven-black hair.
He wears strong light grey worsted clothes because
his work is dusty: he is a stone-mason and walks
three miles to his employers in the market town.
He dislikes living in the hamlet and considers
himself better than his neighbours.*

*ALBERT looks round for his dinner basket but
can't see it. He calls upstage to his wife EMMA.*

ALBERT: Emmie! Emmie!
EMMA: Ssh! . . .
ALBERT: Where's my dinner basket?
EMMA: You'll waken up Laura and Edmund.
ALBERT: Oh, they be up and gone out, woman.

*(EMMA comes downstairs. She is graceful and
her copper-coloured hair hangs loose. She once
was a nursemaid in a good family)*

EMMA: Gone out? Where? Are they after mush-
rooms again?
ALBERT: Aye.
EMMA: Those fields are soaked with dew.
ALBERT: Aye.

EMMA: Six shillingsworth of good shoe-leather
gone for sixpennorth of mushrooms!
ALBERT: He's quick as a flash is our Edmund.
EMMA: Course he is.
ALBERT: We must apprentice him to a good trade.
Carpenters, perhaps. A man with a good trade's
sure of his living.

*(EMMA has found the packed dinner basket and
gives it to him)*

EMMA: You won't stay late tonight will you? Not
again?
ALBERT: Stay late? With the likes of you waiting?

(He kisses her. Their mutual attraction is strong)

What was it that gentleman called you when you
worked at the big house? Pocket Venus, wasn't it?
EMMA: Quite nicely, Albert. He was married with
no nonsense about him.

(They smile and kiss again)

ALBERT: I think we'll give notice on this place, eh?
Move over to Candleford.
EMMA: Aye.
ALBERT: When the old pig's killed I'll give notice.
EMMA: Aye.
ALBERT: Can't never move with an old pig, can
we?
EMMA: No.

*(ALBERT is ready. He picks up his dinner basket,
his apron and tools, and slaps on his billycock hat)*

ALBERT: How do I look, eh? Like a proper
stonemason, eh?

EMMA: You won't stop late, Albert?
ALBERT: I told you, woman.

(His burst of temper and grievance upsets EMMA. But she determines not to part badly)

EMMA: Now let's not part bad. Let's not make it like Dick's hatband, that went half way round and tucked.

(ALBERT too wants to part well. He sighs and gently kisses her)

ALBERT: You go back up, Emma, and have your beauty sleep.

(ALBERT steps outside the house. All over the hamlet men are coming out of their cottages.

They are farm labourers. The young men have drooping walrus moustaches, the elders a fringe of grey whisker beneath the jaw, extending from ear to ear. One or two old men still have smocks and round black felt hats but most wear corduroy trousers and an unbleached drill jacket called a "Sloppy". Some have rush-plaited hats and some billycocks.

BILL MILLER (nicknamed "BISHIE") meets DICK TUFFREY (nicknamed "BOAMER") and his father old DAVID TUFFREY)

BISHIE: Morning, Boamer. Morning, Master Tuffrey.
BOAMER: Morning, Bishie.
OLD DAVID: Morning, young Bill.

(TOM GASKIN nicknamed "PUMPKIN" comes out of his cottage)

BOAMER: Morning, Pumpkin.
PUMPKIN: Morning, lads.
BISHIE: Think weather's a-gooin' to hold?
PUMPKIN: Till us get 'un all in?
BISHIE: Aye.
PUMPKIN: Aye.
OLD DAVID: 'Course it's a-gooin' to hold.

(ALBERT walks in the opposite direction, towards the town. He would pass the men without speaking and they know it. They nudge each other and point)

BISHIE: Look 'ee who's here.
BOAMER: Think he'll not speak nor nothin'?
BISHIE: No. Not him.

(ALBERT walks past them without speaking. Then PUMPKIN calls after him)

PUMPKIN: Morning, Mr Timms.

(ALBERT stops and turns)

ALBERT: Tom Gaskin?
PUMPKIN: Aye.
ALBERT: Morning. Morning all.
OLD DAVID: Morning.
ALBERT: Morning.

(ALBERT manages a nod and a smile for OLD DAVID. Then he strides off)

BISHIE: Now let me ask you, Master Tuffrey — did you ever in all your draggin'-up see a man so stinking with pride?

BOAMER: Bricklayer calling himself a stonemason.

OLD DAVID: Say what you will, I respect his missus.

PUMPKIN: Aye. Oh aye. But all same, she says his family kept an hotel in Oxford: but my wife's cousin knowed fer a fac' it weren't more nor a pot-house.

(The men laugh.

OLD PRICE appears from his house)

OLD PRICE: Morning, David.

OLD DAVID: Morning.

OLD PRICE: Morning, boys.

BOAMER: Morning, Master Price. Think weather's a-gooin' to hold?

OLD PRICE: Till we get 'um in? Course it's a-gooin' to hold.

PUMPKIN: It'll hold fer you, Master Price, what's seen a few harvests in your time.

OLD PRICE: I have Pumpkin: and I hope I'll see a girt lot more.

(Laughter)

BISHIE: Look us all here now. Bailiff's a-waitin'.

(Other men are congregating in the yard of the manor farm. The BAILIFF, MR MORRIS, is a tall, shrivelled, nutcracker-faced old fellow swishing an ash stick. The men call him "Old Monday Morning")

MORRIS: Hi men! Ho men! Monday morning. What do you reckon you're doing?

PUMPKIN: They're all a-coomin' up Muster Morris!

VOICES: Morning, Sam. Morning, Cockie.
MORRIS: Monday morning! Hi men! Ho men! Be
ye deaf or be ye hard of hearing, dang ye! Hurry
up, men!
BISHIE: Hark at old Monday Morning!
MORRIS: Hi men! Ho! Call this harvest morning?
Today's Monday, tomorrow's Tuesday, next
day's Wednesday — half the week gone and
nothing done!
FISHER: Us've harnessed every team up, Muster
Morris!

*(As MORRIS turns his back to look at FISHER,
BOAMER points at him with one hand and with
the other slaps his own buttocks)*

BOAMER: My elbow to you, you old devil!
MORRIS: What's that? What's that?
BOAMER: Just a-asking this little gallass here
what's the matter, Muster Morris.

(The gallass is a youth nicknamed FISHER)

FISHER: Got my boots wet, Boamer — now 'um
dried as stiff as boards.
OLD PRICE: Boots? Good thing you didn't live
when breeches were made o' leather.
BISHIE: Have patience. Remember Job.

(Laughter)

FISHER: Job? What did he know 'bout patience?
He didn't have to wear no leather breeches.

*(His quickness draws a mildly jeering response.
Then a latecomer arrives)*

PUMPKIN: Here's Old Stut late for his own funeral
. . . Morning Stut.

OLD STUT: M-M-Morning, P-P-Pumpkin.

MORRIS: Hi men! Ho men! Now men! We'll put the mechanical reaper in Gibbard's Piece. Will your boots stop you driving the team, young Fisher?

MUTTERED VOICES: (PUMPKIN) Wooman's work! (BOAMER) Well — he's nothin' nor a boychap! (BISHIE) He's young Job!

FISHER: I'll see what I can do Muster Morris, sir.

MORRIS: I'll send the women's gang to bind up after you. Mrs Spicer! Ho! Mrs Spicer!

(MRS SPICER, the leader of the women's gang is formidable in a pair of her husband's corduroy trousers)

MRS SPICER: Here I be Muster Morris!

MORRIS: Hi there! Ho there! What?

OLD PRICE: Speak up, Mrs Spicer.

MRS. SPICER: Eh?

FISHER: Monday Morning can't hear you.

OLD PRICE: You're as hoarse as a crow.

PUMPKIN: As ugly as sin more like.

MRS SPICER: You rub your mouth with salt young Pumpkin!

(The men thoroughly appreciate this exchange)

MORRIS: Gibbard's Piece, Mrs Spicer! Gibbard's Piece! Now men. Hi men! We'll set to with the scythes in Hundred Acre Field. What d'you think of that?

BISHIE: Set us more than us can do and us'll do it!

PUMPKIN: You'll not never need them jibberin' old Irish gypsies this year Muster Morris!

MORRIS: Farmer and his wife have provided some good ale as usual and I'll be riding round with it! I'll be riding, men! Have you chosen your King of the Mowers?

ALL: Aye! We have that! Aye!
MORRIS: Who is it?
BISHIE: Boamer!

(Cheers and a bit of backslapping)

OLD PRICE: Wert up, Boamer lad!
BOAMER: Thank God for having growed the corn
up right Muster Morris, for us'll bring 'un down
all right, eh, boys?
ALL: That us will! Good old Boamer!
MORRIS: You lead the line, Boamer. You say when
they rest. You say what drinks they take. Monday
Morning! Ho there! Hi there!
OLD PRICE: Come on Boamer, lad. On with your
hat then!

(They cheer and lift him up)

BOAMER: Follow me, lads, for I'm your King of
the Mowers!

(They carry him off as they sing)

HARVEST WORK SONG

When harvest come on and the reaping begins
The farmer the fruit of the earth gathers in.
In mirth let us talk till the season be gone
And at night give a holla till it's all of a row,
    till it's all of a row,
And at night give a holla till it's all of a row.

Then early next morning our hooks we do
    grind,
And away to the cornfields to reap and to bind.
Our foreman looks back and he leaves well behind,
And he gives a loud holla bring it all well
    behind, bring it all well behind,

And he gives a loud holla bring it all well
   behind.

Oh then says the foreman behind and before
We will have a fresh whet and a half a pint
   more.
So me jolly boys to the end we will go,
To the end we will go till it's all of a row, till it's
   all of a row,
To the end we will go till it's all of a row.

When night it comes on to the farm we will
   steer,
To partake a good supper and to drink a strong
   beer,
In wishing the farmer such blessings in his life,
And in drinking a health unto him and his wife,
   unto him and his wife,
And in drinking a health unto him and his wife.

Our wheat is all in, oats barley are bound,
Here's success to the farmer who ploughs
   through the ground,
As for this wheat stubble into turnips we'll sew,
And so we'll continue till it's all of a row, till
   it's all of a row,
   And so we'll continue till it's all of a row.

(Last refrain repeated as necessary)

Scene 2
BREAKFAST

*LAURA and EDMUND have returned to the end
house and both they and their mother are enjoying
the fried mushrooms. EMMA is dressed now and
her hair is parted in the middle and drawn down to*

*a knot at the back. The children do not speak
while eating.*

EMMA: Edmund. Sit up, Edmund!

(EDMUND sits up)

Six shillingsworth of good shoe-leather gone for
six-pennorth of mushrooms!

(LAURA opens her mouth)

Little girls should be seen and not heard.

(Her mother's finger and eyebrows go up)

Don't speak while you're eating.

*(LAURA does not speak. She returns to her
mushrooms. LAURA finishes. She looks at
EDMUND. He is still eating. Then EDMUND
finishes. Their mother looks at them:*

Now what d'you do?

*LAURA folds her hands to say grace. EDMUND
follows suit)*

LAURA: Thank God for my good breakfast. Thank
father and mother. Amen.
EDMUND: Amen.
EMMA: Amen.
LAURA: I didn't wear no boots and gave Edmund
my old ones.
EMMA: Going out without boots? You must be
cold as ice.

*(Silence. LAURA and her mother have not quite
made it up)*

EDMUND: Mother.
EMMA: What?
EDMUND: What's the sea like?
EMMA: It's big, Edmund. Now don't go asking me
questions.

*(Mother starts to clear the table. LAURA helps
her)*

EDMUND: Is it as big as Cottesloe Pond?
EMMA: Good Lord, yes.
EDMUND: How far away is it? Is it as far as
Oxford?
LAURA: You've seen maps.
EDMUND: No I haven't.
LAURA: I have.
EMMA: See what I've done, Laura? See what I've
saved fer your father? Your two biggest
mushrooms — 'cause of how he likes 'em so.

*(LAURA smiles. She and her mother embrace
each other for a moment. There is happy peace
between them)*

EDMUND: Mother. What's Oxford like?
EMMA: It's a girt big town where you can earn five
and twenty shilling a week and pay pretty near
half in rent so who'd want to go?
EDMUND: What do people do there?
EMMA: It's full of old buildings. It's where rich
people's sons go to school when they're grown up.
EDMUND: What do they learn?
EMMA: Latin and Greek and suchlike I suppose.
EDMUND: Do they all go there?
EMMA: No. Some go to Cambridge.
EDMUND: Which shall I go to when I grow up?
EMMA: You'll have to go to work, my little man.
Brains ain't no good to a working chap. They

make him discontented and saucy and lose him jobs.

(EMMA takes her mats and rugs outside the cottage and beats them. Other women are doing the same)

Morning, Mrs Blaby.
MRS BLABY: Morning, Mrs Timms.
EMMA: Morning, Mrs Peverill.
MRS PEVERILL: Morning.
EMMA: Think the weather's going to hold?
MRS BLABY: Until they get 'un all in?
EMMA: Aye.
MRS PEVERILL: Bound to, my husband says.

(EDMUND watches his mother at work)

EDMUND: Mother: why does God sometimes send bad weather?
EMMA: Questions, Edmund, questions! You may not have school to go to but I've still to beat and scrub so go play while you can. Laura. Go play with him.

(LAURA and EDMUND wander past the hard-working women)

LAURA: Oh look! What's that plant called Mrs Peverill?
MRS PEVERILL: 'Tis called mind your own business, and I think I'd better give a slip of it to your mother to pot up for you.

(LAURA wheels the gird away. EDMUND follows)

Ask me I'd say children should be seen and not heard.

MRS BLABY: Time she was earning her own living.
MRS PEVERILL: Come next harvest she will be.
MRS BLABY: Not much to look at is she: like a moll
heron, all legs and wings.

Scene 3
OLD SALLY AND DICK

*OLD SALLY comes out of her cottage. She is a
tall, broad old woman, eighty years old, with dark
curls and a white fringed cap.*

SALLY: Laura! Laura! Coom up here!
LAURA: It's Old Sally. Come on.

(The children go up to Old Sally)

Morning Sally.
SALLY: Morning Laura.

*(Sally's husband DICK is there, a dry little
withered old man with a smock rolled up round
his waist and trousers gartered with buckled
straps. SALLY is by far the dominating partner
but DICK is gleefully happy)*

LAURA: Morning, Dick.
DICK: Morning, Laura.
LAURA: Oh Sally what a good smell!
SALLY: I been brewin' haven't I?
EDMUND: Oh Laura, look at those roses!
DICK: York and Lancaster, they call 'em. Them's
better'n any o' yer oil paintin's. Eh?
SALLY: Dick. Show young Edmund here the
grandfather clock.
EDMUND: Oh please!
DICK: Oh. Aye. Just as Sally says! Come on, only
grandfather clock in the Rise.

(LAURA is not sure whether to follow DICK and EDMUND or not. SALLY motions her to stay)

SALLY: Laura. You'm a good girl and I likes you. I know you'm good at readin' and writin' on account of how folks tries to pluck your feathers.
LAURA: But Dick can write can't he?
SALLY: Oh he could write ten words to us boys when they was in India and I can make my name and that be all so it's a bit okkard for business.

(Silence. SALLY watches LAURA)

Laura, ask me I'd say you'm a girl might keep a secret.
LAURA: Oh yes. Oh, yes, Sally.
SALLY: What do folk say 'bout me and Dick.

(LAURA hesitates)

Go on! Don't flinch!
LAURA: They say they wish you'd tell them how 'tis done. How you live so comfortable when you're so old.

(SALLY laughs and clasps her hands)

SALLY: Laura: when I were your age, all the land between here and the church were left by will to the poor o' the parish. All common land of turf and fuzz 'twas then. But 'twere all stole away an' cut up into fields. Hundred Acre Field were common land. My grandfather owned this house and passed it on to my father. Us had a cow and pigs and a donkey cart and I drove the geese to the common. I know'd where the freshest grass growed I can tell you. Us growed us own victuals and my mother made butter and at harvest time an' such like my dad worked for wages. So us was happy. Not like country folk today, eh, raising great tribes o' children on ten shillin' a week wages. I didn't never hold wi' havin' a lot o' poor brats an' nothin' to put in their bellies. Took us all us time to bring up us two and us hand —

(SALLY checks. She has reached the point of the conversation)

Us be swearin' you to secrecy, Laura.

(LAURA nods vigorously. Trust me)

Well. A-cause my father had a share o' common land he could make summat. And a-cause he made summat he left summat. He left this house and seventy-five pound!

(LAURA gasps)

Aye. An' me and Dick has saved every week for sixty year even if it were no more nor a penny nor twopence. So that's how 'tis done.
LAURA: But why tell *me*, Sally?
SALLY: 'Cause we need letters writ to seedsmen, an' postal orders fetched an' money added up. It be growed into more 'n poor old Dick's head can reckon. I watched him t'other night, poor old boy. It were like puttin' a poultice on a wooden leg. Will you help us?
LAURA: Yes. Can I? Oh yes! *(They embrace)*
SALLY: Dick. Dick. Here, Laura. Take your mother a bunch o' rosemary.

(DICK and EDMUND return)

EDMUND: Oh Laura, it's such a big clock, but the moon's broken.

DICK: Aye, but we be a' bed early so we don't miss him. Will 'er do it?
SALLY: Aye.
DICK: I were a cat on hot bricks in there.

(SALLY gives LAURA the rosemary)

SALLY: Here. Come tomorrow morning. Quick sharp.

(LAURA and EDMUND go. SALLY and DICK wave after them. LAURA and EDMUND wave and then walk on)

LAURA: Edmund. Guess what!
EDMUND: What?
LAURA: When Sally was like me she was a goose-girl!

(The band sings and plays):

YOUNG SALLY'S SONG

Come Sally young Sally and call the geese home
Call Lizzie call Dripping call Waddle-down-by
There's a great big black cloud full of snow in the sky
Come Sally young Sally and drive the geese home

Where's Sally young Sally who called the geese home
Where's Lizzie where's Dripping where's Waddle-down-by
Where are all the cold hailstones that fell from the sky
Where's Sally young Sally who drove the geese home

Oh Sally old Sally who called the geese home
Where's Lizzie where's Dripping who cackled
   all day
All gone like the fields that were stolen away
And Sally young Sally who drove the geese
   home

All gone like the fields that were stolen away
And Sally young Sally who drove the geese
   home.

Scene 4
TEN O'CLOCK POST

*EMMA has done her scrubbing and emptied the
fireplace which she is now cleaning, watched by
LAURA and EDMUND.*

EMMA: See this grate I'm cleaning? Looks done,
doesn't it? But you watch.

(She brushes vigorously)

There. That's the secret. Just that bit of extra
elbow grease after some folks would consider a
thing done.
LAURA: Oh mother! Post, mother! Here's Old
Postie!

*(EMMA and other women come out of their
houses. OLD POSTIE is a gloomy, grumpy man
with flat feet. He has been forty years on this
round and walks with deliberate, rheumatic
slowness)*

EMMA: Look at him dawdle! You expecting
something, Mrs Peverill?

MRS PEVERILL: No, I be-ant expecting nothing but I be so yarning.

(OLD POSTIE stops, looks through the letters and small parcels, and speaks to the women outside the group of cottages)

OLD POSTIE: No, I ain't got nothing for you, Mrs Peverill. Your young Annie wrote to you only last week. She's got summat else to do besides sitting down on her arse in the servant's kitchen writin' home all the time.
MRS PEVERILL: I call that real forrard language.
OLD POSTIE: Mrs Blaby. Parcel!
EMMA: Mrs Blaby!

(MRS BLABY comes out of her cottage)

MRS BLABY: It's not summat for me is it?
OLD POSTIE: 'Tis from your Aggie in London. Sent you her best dress I'll be bound.
MRS BLABY: Well, better be out of the world than out of the fashion, b'ain't that what they say?
OLD POSTIE: Oh, there is one for you, Mrs Peverill! And my! Ain't it a thin-roed 'un. Not much time to write to her mother these days. I took a good fat 'un from her to young Chad Gubbins.
MRS PEVERILL: Oh! — Don't he leave a sting behind him!

(OLD POSTIE waddles on. The women return to their homes. EMMA takes her mats in with her)

EDMUND: Mother, why are people in Lark Rise so poor?
EMMA: Poverty's no disgrace, Edmund, but 'tis a great inconvenience.

(LAURA has seen something in the distance and points)

LAURA: What's that?
EMMA: Where?
LAURA: Coming from the turnpike.
EMMA: Oh, yes. I see him. Driving too quick to be the fish cart.
EDMUND: It's the doctor's gig.
EMMA: So it is.
LAURA: Is anybody sick?
EMMA: If they were we'd have had the gossips round by this time in the morning — and Mrs Beamish hasn't come to her time yet.
EDMUND: He must be going to Fordlow.
EMMA: Aye. *(Her mind goes on to the next thing)* Now Laura, you run round the Rise to poor Mr Sharman, there's a good girl, and ask him could he fancy a bite of cold bacon for his dinner.

(LAURA goes to the cottage of SHARMAN, who is known as the Major because he served in the army. He is old and ill and has just dressed and with great difficulty dragged his chair to the fire)

LAURA: Mr Sharman! Morning, Mr Sharman.
SHARMAN: Uh? Oh. It's you, Laura.
LAURA: My mother says could you fancy a bit of bacon for your dinner?
SHARMAN: I'm cold.
LAURA: Sun's shining, Mr Sharman.
SHARMAN: I'm cold.

(The DOCTOR and the LOCAL CARRIER have got out of the gig. They walk past the end house)

EMMA: Morning, Doctor.
DOCTOR: Morning, Mrs Timms.

EMMA: No trouble I hope?
DOCTOR: No, no. We've just come for Mr
Sharman.
EMMA: Oh no!

(EMMA knows exactly what they mean)

SHARMAN: Dunno where I'd be without your
mum, Laura.
LAURA: Would you fancy some bacon?
SHARMAN: I had bacon every day in the army.
LAURA: What shall I tell her then?
SHARMAN: I'm cold.
LAURA: It's coming up very hot, Mr Sharman.

(The DOCTOR and the CARRIER march in)

DOCTOR: Morning, Major. Come along now.
SHARMAN: Eh? What?
DOCTOR: It's a nice morning. We've come to take
you for a drive.
SHARMAN: A drive? I've not driven nowhere since
I left the hospital. Where to?
DOCTOR: Oh, just a drive.
SHARMAN: You'd not put me in the workhouse?
DOCTOR: You'll feel better for the sunshine.
SHARMAN: I won't go. I can look after myself.
DOCTOR: No you can't, and you've no family to
do it for you.
SHARMAN: I'm a soldier. I'll not die in no work-
house.
DOCTOR: Come along, old chap.

*(They lift SHARMAN up. He tries to resist but is
too weak. They hustle his coat round his
shoulders)*
SHARMAN: Let me be.
DOCTOR: That's the way. Put your shawl on.

(The band sings)

JOHN BARLEYCORN

There were three men come out of the West,
The victory to try,
And these three men they made a vow,
John Barleycorn should die.

They ploughed, they sowed, they harrowed
    them in,
Throwed clods all on his head,
And these three men rejoicing went,
John Barleycorn was dead.

They rode him round and round the field,
Till they came into a barn,
And there they made a solemn mow,
On little John Barleycorn.

They hired men with the crab tree sticks,
To cut him skin from bone,
But the miller he served him worse than that,
For he ground him between two stones.

DOCTOR: It's all for the best.

(Everyone sings)

All good gifts around us,
Are sent from heaven above,
So thank the Lord, O thank the Lord,
For all His love.

Scene 5
GRANDFATHER

*Laura's grandfather is a tall, old man with snow
white hair and beard and blue eyes. He wears an*

*old fashioned close-fitting black overcoat and a
bowler hat. He moves slowly and painfully
because rheumatism is gradually seizing up his
joints. He is carrying a gift of freshly-cut flowers
from his garden.*

*To reach the end house GRANDFATHER must
pass Queenie's cottage. QUEENIE MACEY is a
little, wrinkled, yellow-faced old woman in a lilac
sunbonnet. She is sitting on a chair. She is dozing
in the sun.*

GRANDFATHER: Morning Twister, Morning
Queenie, and how are you this — fast asleep, God
bless her.

*(Queenie's husband TWISTER pops up from
behind the hedge. He is a small, thin-legged,
jackdaw-eyed old fellow dressed in an old
velveteen coat that once belonged to a gamekeeper,
a peacock's feather stuck in the band of his
battered old bowler, and a red and yellow
handkerchief knotted under one ear. He too has
rheumatism and is slowly becoming the slack-
witted person that he has often pretended to be.
He has a big open clasp-knife in one hand)*

TWISTER: Why should God bless her? Why should
he? I'll wake 'un up fer 'ee.
GRANDFATHER: No need for that, Twister, thank
'ee kindly.
TWISTER: Her be my wife and un'll do what I says.
GRANDFATHER: What was you a-doing behind
that hedge?
TWISTER: Nothing. I caught a frog. Sun's shining
ain't it?
GRANDFATHER: You let that frog go, Twister,
d'you hear?

TWISTER: I did. I did let 'un go. But first I cut him front legs off.

(TWISTER thinks that this is both daring and funny)

GRANDFATHER: Lord have mercy, Twister. Lord have mercy.

(GRANDFATHER walks slowly on. EMMA sees him and goes to meet him)

EMMA: Why, father: you've not walked round the Rise for a week or more.

(GRANDFATHER gives her the flowers)

Oh, dad. From your garden? Thank you. It just makes me think if only I had thirty shillings a week regular I could keep everything so nice and tidy and keep *such* a table.

(GRANDFATHER sits painfully. EMMA gets a flower jar)

GRANDFATHER: Poor old Twister, eh? Poor Twister.
EMMA: There's some thinks he'd be better put away — but there he is, he still goes beating at shoots and he still earns a shilling or two opening farm gates for the brewery salesman's gig.
GRANDFATHER: I've knowed him forty year and he was allus the same. Whatever he dies on, he won't kill hisself with hard work. *(He notices that something is wrong)* Emmie? Emmie, you b'ain't crying be you?
EMMA: Oh, father.

(EMMA weeps. Then she hears the children, she pulls herself together.

LAURA and EDMUND come in)

LAURA: Oh mother. Mother, they've taken Mr Sharman away.

EMMA: I know. I saw them.

GRANDFATHER: We all saw 'em — except your granny. She wouldn't look.

LAURA: Why not? What was she doing?

GRANDFATHER: Reading.

EDMUND: What? What was she reading?

EMMA: Don't ask questions!

GRANDFATHER: Now, Emmie . . . She were reading one of those what-d'you-call-'ems, Edmund — novelettes. All about dukes and duchesses. When you say your prayers tonight ask the Lord to help Mr Sharman.

EDMUND: D'you ever pray for your old fiddle?

GRANDFATHER: My old fiddle?

EDMUND: Didn't that get taken away?

LAURA: It had to be sold when granny was ill.

GRANDFATHER: I got five pound for it.

LAURA: Did you miss it?

GRANDFATHER: I did, my maid, more than anything I've ever had to part with, and that's not a little, and I miss it still and always shall. But it went for a good cause and we can't have everything we want in this world. It wouldn't be good for us.

LAURA: Why not? I'd call it very good for you to have your old fiddle.

EMMA: Laura. Don't answer back.

LAURA: It's always money that causes people's troubles.

EMMA: Laura!

GRANDFATHER: If it *were* just money, Laura, life 'ud be simple.

EMMA: Now then Laura, here's a penny. You go wait for Jerry Parish and you buy three oranges.

(The children are delighted. They rush out)

I'm sorry, father. They've so many questions.
GRANDFATHER: They'll find answers in the Bible and their own good time.

(EMMA smiles. She admires her father's religious faith without being able to share it so deeply)

EMMA: How's your rheumatics?
GRANDFATHER: Bad.
EMMA: Is this walk too much for you?

(GRANDFATHER gestures. He does not want to admit it easily, but the walk is too far)

I'll visit you. You save yourself for your garden.
GRANDFATHER: It's run wild since I can't stoop so much.

(Silence)

Your uncle's well. He sends you kind regards.

EMMA: He's a good man.
GRANDFATHER: To send me money? Aye. He is.
EMMA: But you'd send it to him if you'd prospered.

(GRANDFATHER watches her)

GRANDFATHER: What about you, Emmie? Do you prosper?

(EMMA shakes her head)

EMMA: Every year Albert says we'll give notice and move to Candleford. We'll go when we've killed the pig he says, then when we've killed the pig he'll say we'll go at Michaelmas. But we won't.
GRANDFATHER: Do you want to leave the Rise?
EMMA: I want him to be happy. I don't want him always coming home late from public houses.

(EMMA almost cries again)

EMMA: You're good to me, father. You're so good.
GRANDFATHER: Well, you've always brought me your troubles, haven't you?

(EMMA kneels in front of him: a little girl again.

GRANDFATHER smiles and, a bit awkwardly because of his rheumatism, wipes her eyes)

EMMA: Oh, father . . .
GRANDFATHER: Sssh . . .
EMMA: I'm sorry. I don't want to flinch.

(EMMA blows her nose)

GRANDFATHER: That's better. That's better. Now, you're going to be my own brave little wench. And remember, my dear, there's One above who knows what's best for use, even though we may not see it ourselves at the time.

(EMMA kisses him. There is great love between them)

Now help me up.

(EMMA helps him up. It hurts. He smiles ruefully. He starts to go)

EMMA: How long did you have that violin, father?
GRANDFATHER: Oh — fifty year. It's no use to me
now. My fingers is too stiff to play it.

(He seems to be going but turns again)

Of course, when I bought it I was still a sinner. I
hadn't seen Jesus face to face. I were an eggler of
course but I didn't have the horse. I walked to buy
eggs and carry 'em to market. Oh, I strode out,
Emmie. I was a brisk young sinner I can tell you
and I'd take my fiddle and play it at fairs. Folks
'ud dance and sing all night and I'd laugh and play
for 'em all night!

*(GRANDFATHER shakes his head and walks
slowly away to the accompaniment of a lively
fiddle tune)*

Scene 6
TOMMYTOES

*(JERRY PARISH enters with his fish and fruit
cart. Women of the village come to meet him)*

JERRY: Bloaters a penny each; oranges three a
penny.
MRS PEVERILL: I've threepence till my man gets his
money.
JERRY: Have a bloater.
MRS PEVERILL: But I've the children, Jerry. Mind
you, I've some bread. Show me one wi' plenty of
soft roes. I could spread it for them.
MRS BEAMISH: Morning, Jerry.
JERRY: Morning, Mrs Beamish. Gor' blime me!
Never knowed such a lot in my life for soft roes.
Good job I ain't soft-roed or I should have got
eaten up myself afore now! *(He feels bloater)*
Oozin' — simply oozin' with goodness I tell ye!

But what's the good of one bloater among the lot
of ye! Tell you what I'll do. I'll put you in these
three whoppers for twopence-halfpenny.

MRS PEVERILL: No.

JERRY: Tell you what. Have three oranges.
When you've eaten 'em dry the peel on the
hob, then the children chews on it or swops it
for conkers.

MRS PEVERILL: No, Jerry. If I've any money over
I've got to put it to a new pair of boots for our
George.

JERRY: Lor blime me, Mrs Peverill. I don't know
why you come out here!

MRS PEVERILL: To have a look and a bit of a chat,
Jerry. Why else?

MRS MILLER: I'll have a bloater.

JERRY: What's that? Mrs Miller?

MRS MILLER: I've worked that hard this morning. I
just fancy a bit o'summat.

JERRY: This bloater's more'n a bit, Mrs Miller. It's
three happorth worth for a penny.

(It is now LAURA's turn)

LAURA: Oh look Edmund! Mr Parish, what are
those red things?

JERRY: Love apples, my dear. Love apples they be,
although some hignorant folks be a-calling them
tommytoes. But you don't want any o'they —
nasty sour things they be, as only gentry can eat.

LAURA: They look beautiful.

JERRY: They'll only make 'ee sick. What's it to be?
Three oranges?

LAURA: Please. Oh. What's that?

JERRY: That fish? That's a John Dory, my dear.
See them black marks? Look like finger marks
don't 'em? An' they do say that they be finger
marks. *He* made 'em, that night, ye know, when

they was fishin', ye know, and *He* took some and
cooked 'em all ready for 'em an' ever since they
say that ivery John Dory as comes out of the sea
have got *HIS* finger marks on 'em.
LAURA: Do you mean the Sea of Galilee?
JERRY: That's it, my dear. That's what they say;
whether true or not of course I *don't* know, but
there be the finger marks right enough, and that's
what they say in our trade.

OLD JERRY'S SONG

Band:
Are you there John Dory
Are you there
In Cottesloe Pond?
Are you there in glory
Are you there
In Cottesloe Pond?
Are you there?

Jerry:
I've red tommytoes for the gentry
I've bloaters for the likes of you
I've pears and I've peaches a-plenty
And an orange for the likes of you

I've a bunch of grapes for the gentry
And bloaters for the likes of you
I can tip my hat most politely
An be patient with the likes of you

There's one kind of fish that is saintly
And he's taught me a thing or two
It's red tommytoes for the gentry
And patience for the likes of you

All:
Yes it's red tommytoes for the gentry
And it's patience for the likes of us!

Band:
Are you there John Dory
Are you there
In Cottesloe Pond?
Are you there in glory
Are you there
In Cottesloe Pond?

Are you there John Dory
Are you there
In Cottesloe Pond?
Are you there in glory
Are you there
In Cottesloe Pond?
Are you there John Dory
Are you there?

END OF ACT ONE

ACT TWO

Scene 1
MID-DAY. QUEENIE

OLD TWISTER, realising that QUEENIE is still asleep and that EMMA is alone again, sidles up to the end house and calls her.

TWISTER: Hey, missis. Missis Timms.

(EMMA jumps)

Did you know that twenty year ago I used to sell nuts on market days?
EMMA: Yes. Queenie told me.
TWISTER: Bassalonie nuts. Do you want to see 'em?
EMMA: How can I see them, Twister, if it was twenty years ago?
TWISTER: Oh you can see 'em, missis. Here they be!

(TWISTER lets his trousers fall and exposes himself)

Bassalonies big as ponies!

EMMA: Twister, you ought to be ashamed of yourself doing that again.
TWISTER: Bassalonies big as ponies!

(QUEENIE wakes up)

QUEENIE: Twister! You disgusting old fool, you!

(TWISTER is dismayed. He clutches at his trousers and runs away)

Look at him. Slack-twisted old fool. Run away at
the sight of me. As well as might. Still remembers
the pie, don't he? Did I tell 'ee about the pie?
EMMA: You did Queenie, but it can bear telling
again.
QUEENIE: Well. 'Twere forty-five year ago. He
came home drunk and took the strap off his
trousers and he beat me. I went to bed sobbin' I
did. Next morning he gets up but no strap. Not
nowhere to be found. So he holds his trousers up
wi' string and goes to work. Well — when he come
home for tea I'd baked a pie. I'd done a tulip on
top and it were baked just beautiful. "You cut it
up," I says, "I made it a-purpose for you. Come,
don't 'ee be afraid of it. 'Tis all for you." Then I
turns my back on him and looks in the cupboard
and he cuts the pie and there inside on it is the
strap all curled up. Twister just went white as a
ghost an' got up an' went out. But it cured 'em
for's not so much as laid a finger on me from that
day to this! And I hope a-Saturday he comes home
wi' a shillin' or two for if he don't there be no tea
for him and no snuff for me neither.

(QUEENIE takes out her snuffbox)

Look at 'un. Clean empty and I can't do wi'out
my pinch o'snuff. 'Tis meat an' drink to me.

(QUEENIE sniffs deeply at the empty box)

Ah! That's better. The ghost o' good snuff's
better nor nothing. Mrs Timms, my dear, if I had
a pound a week coming in I 'udn't care if it rained
hatchets and hammers!

(QUEENIE and EMMA laugh)

EMMA: How are the bees, Queenie?
QUEENIE: Poor little craturs.
EMMA: You ain't still waiting for the last swarm?
QUEENIE: I am. They was almost frozed in winter.
I wanted to gather them up, take them indoors,
and set them in rows in front of a good fire, and
then there were all that rain and as you know Mrs
Timms a swarm in July ain't worth a fly so I'll not
have too much for the honey-man. That's why I
need Twister, for all his disgustin' carrin'-ons.
Come winter I'll need every shillin' he can earn.

(They both start at the noise they hear)

QUEENIE: That's it. That's the little craturs
swarming.
EMMA: There they go. Down your sweet-pea alley.

*(QUEENIE rushes home and picks up her pitch
fork and an iron spoon)*

Queenie. Hurry, Queenie. They're buzzing over
into Master Tuffrey's.

*(QUEENIE rushes after the bees, tanging the
spoon on the back of the pitch-fork)*

QUEENIE: I'm after 'em Mrs Timms. I'm after
'em!

Scene 2
MRS BEAMISH

*Martha's mother MRS BEAMISH is heavily
pregnant. During the following scene MRS
BEAMISH plaits Martha's long hair into an
inverted saucer at the back of her head. LAURA*

watches and EDMUND stands where he can
follow what is happening but not be part of it.

MRS BEAMISH: Martha, will you please keep still!
Now you know where the big house is don't you,
Martha?
MARTHA: I can ask on the way.
MRS BEAMISH: It's four miles walking. And when
you get there you speak proper and you answer
"Yes, mum" all polite like. Keep still!
MARTHA: "Yes, mum". How will it look?
MRS BEAMISH: Like a scarecrow if you don't keep
still.
LAURA: Have you had it plaited up before,
Martha?

(MARTHA shakes her head excitedly)

MRS BEAMISH: Keep still, Martha! And don't go
undoing it on the way nor nothing like that. You
say you're Martha Beamish and you're twelve
years old and you've just left school and you're
looking for your petty place to learn service in. It's
a big house. It's not a farmhouse. Once a
farmhouse servant allus a farmhouse servant but
this is a big house and you'll be growing strong
enough for proper gentlemen's service. Understand?
MARTHA: Yes, ma. How do I look?
MRS BEAMISH: You'll see soon enough. If I hadn't
felt sick as a dog this morning I would have come
with you even if my time is near.
MARTHA: I know you would, ma.
MRS BEAMISH: How about asking Laura if she'll
go with you? Keep still. It's company isn't it?
MARTHA: Oh, can I ma? Would you like that,
Laura?
LAURA: Yes.

MRS BEAMISH: Will it suit your mother?

LAURA: Yes.

MRS BEAMISH: What you *must* do, Martha, and you must see as she does, Laura, is when the lady asks you say I've not a penny to spend on your outfit.

MARTHA: Not a penny.

MRS BEAMISH: So will her send me your first month's wages in a-hadvance to buy necessaries. Understand?

MARTHA: Yes.

MRS BEAMISH: Laura?

LAURA: Yes. I'd best go for my dinner now.

MRS BEAMISH: Aye. You had.

MARTHA: Oh how do it look, ma?

MRS BEAMISH: Come in and I'll show 'ee.

(EDMUND is waiting for LAURA. They walk along in silence and then he speaks)

EDMUND: Mother won't let you walk four miles.

LAURA: I shan't tell her.

EDMUND: She'll find out.

LAURA: Oh be quiet, Edmund.

EDMUND: I want to go with you.

LAURA: You can't walk that far.

EDMUND: Yes I can. I want to see a big house.

(LAURA is about to admonish him when they see QUEENIE pass by in the distance still tanging her bees. When QUEENIE has disappeared LAURA turns back to EDMUND)

QUEENIE: I'm still after the little craturs. I'm still after them.

LAURA: You can't walk that far.

EDMUND: Shall I ask mother if I can?

(Impasse. LAURA has to give way)

LAURA: Just you keep up with us, that's all.
EDMUND: Course I will. There's the Squire.
LAURA: Where?
EDMUND: There. Going home from his shooting.

Scene 3
SQUIRE BRACEWELL

SQUIRE BRACEWELL has a gun and haversack and a brace of dead rabbits. He is a jovial, red-faced, middle-aged bachelor and lives at the hall with his widowed mother. They are not so well off as they once were. BRACEWELL is a simple, sincere person who is on the whole well-liked in the village and hamlet.

SQUIRE: I say. John Price. It is John Price isn't it?

(JOHN PRICE is a young man in a red infantry jacket. He is a son of OLD DAVID PRICE and has just finished his five years' service in the army)

PRICE: Yes, sir. John Price, sir.
SQUIRE: Just got your discharge?
PRICE: Yes, sir.
SQUIRE: How many years was it?
PRICE: Five.
SQUIRE: Good Lord. I remember you at the schoolroom concert. Five years. Good Lord. You were in the Sudan weren't you?
PRICE: Yes, sir.
SQUIRE: Good Lord.

(There is a little awkward silence)

PRICE: I see you're still out with your gun, sir.
SQUIRE: Oh yes. I never miss a day.
PRICE: I hopes your mother be keeping well, sir.
SQUIRE: Thank you, Price. Thank you. She is.
She's looking older of course, but . . .

(There is another awkward silence)

Speaking of the annual schoolroom concert, you
were one of my stalwarts, you know.
PRICE: I did my bit, sir.
SQUIRE: You were jolly good. I still run the Negro
Minstrel Troupe.
PRICE: I always enjoyed putting black on my face,
sir.
SQUIRE: For the last couple of years we've got up
red and blue uniforms — and we've got a new
song.
PRICE: Oh aye?
SQUIRE: Would you like to hear it?

(SQUIRE BRACEWELL sings):

NEGRO MINSTREL SONG

A friend of Darwin's came to me
"A million years ago" said he
"You had a tail and no great toe"
I answered him "That may be so
But I've one now I'll let you know
G-r-r-r-r-out!"

(SQUIRE makes a kicking motion)

SQUIRE: And then I plant a great kick on Tom
Binns's backside.
PRICE: Tom Binns.
SQUIRE: Yes. People seem to laugh more at him

than at the others. We rehearse once a week in the
schoolroom. Are you going to volunteer again?
PRICE: I be happy to, sir.
SQUIRE: Splendid. Thank you Price. Thank you
kindly. Blackie! Dot! Now where are those
confounded dogs?
PRICE: Er — a friend of who's sir?
SQUIRE: What? Oh. Darwin's. A friend of
Darwin's came to me. Good day.
PRICE: Good day to you, Mr Bracewell, sir.

SOLDIER'S SONG

(as the men return from the fields)

Poor old soldier,
Poor old soldier,
If ever I 'list for a soldier again,
The devil shall be me Sergeant.

Poor old soldier,
Poor old soldier,
If every I 'list for a soldier again,
The devil shall be me Sergeant.

Twopence I got for selling my cloak,
And twopence for selling my blanket,
If ever I 'list for a soldier again,
The devil shall be me Sergeant.

Poor old soldier,
Poor old soldier,
If ever I 'list for a soldier again,
The devil shall be me Sergeant.

Scene 4
MEN AFIELD

The line moves on across the field. Then when
BOAMER raises his hand both the line and the
music stop.

BOAMER: Master Price, what time be it by your old
turnip watch?
OLD PRICE: Ten minutes after, Boamer.
BOAMER: I thought it must be. Knock off for
dinner hour, lads. Sit down and rest your back-
sides. But it won't be no hour. Half hour exact
and then back to it. Now where's Pumpkin with
that yellow-stone jar? Pumpkin! *(answering*
shout) You bring up the jar? *(another shout)* Well
hurry up. And when you do, give the oldest first
drink of ale.

(The men throw themselves down on the ground
and open their lunches. The food is wrapped in
handkerchiefs. Some have bread and cold bacon,
which they cut very neatly with claspknives. Some
have bread and a bit of cheese.

It is eagerly awaited relaxation. The men are
hungry. Their conversation is punctuated by
silences of rest and eating)

OLD PRICE: Well — us've made a good start,
Boamer lad.
BISHIE: Aye. Us have. Good old Boamer.
OLD PRICE: Best start I've seed for twenty year.
BOAMER: We must keep at it and hope that
weather holds.
PUMPKIN: *(Arriving from wheatfield)* What have
you got there, Bishie lad?

(BISHIE holds up a piece of cheese and then pops it into his mouth, PUMPKIN smiles)

You've seen some hard day's work in these fields, Master Tuffrey.

OLD DAVID: Aye.

PUMPKIN: What was the hardest?

OLD DAVID: The hardest?

OLD PRICE: Aye. What *were* the hardest?

OLD DAVID: Oh the hardest were in Duffus Piece when farmer was a young man and he says, says he, "That field o' oats got to come in afore night, for there's a rain a'coming!" But we didn't flinch, not we! Got the last load under cover by midnight. A'most too fagged-out to walk home. But we didn't flinch. We done it!

PUMPKIN: I'll wager you done it, Master Tuffrey.

OLD DAVID: Oh we done it, Pumpkin! We done it!

(Appreciative smiles and chuckles. They eat and pass the ale)

BISHIE: Weren't it Duffus Piece where you a-faced up to the old bull, Master Price?

OLD PRICE: No, that were Fishponds.

BISHIE: O'course it were. Fishponds.

(OLD PRICE rests and reflects. They wait for him to tell the story)

OLD PRICE: Old bull — he comes for me wi' his head down. But I didn't flinch. I ripped off a bit o' loose rail and went for he. 'Twas him as did the flinchin'!

(Warm laughter and then silence)

BISHIE: Now you lads with them cold pudding

ends. Don't be gettin' that 'ere treacle in your
ears.

(The men amused)

OLD DAVID: Pass the jug, Pumpkin, thank 'ee
kindly.
BISHIE: Where's Old Monday Morning with the
barrel?
BOAMER: Oh he be riding round after dinner or I'll
have strong words to say to him.
OLD PRICE: That you will, Boamer.

(Laughter)

You must be proud of him, David. Regular proud
o' a son like him.
OLD DAVID: Oh aye.
BISHIE: Not fagged out are you, Master Tuffrey?
OLD DAVID: Half fagged, Bishie. Half fagged.
PUMPKIN: That's a good 'un. Half fagged!

*(By now the men are finishing their food. They
shake out the crumbs from their red handkerchiefs,
and light their clay pipes with thick shag tobacco)*

BOAMER: Now, you young boychaps — if you
want to walk off and shoot your catapults 'tis the
time to do it. But don't be making no nuisance for
Mrs Spicer's gang and when you hear me a-
shouting come back here.
PUMPKIN: If you ask me, we'd a-get this corn in
faster without them boys.
OLD PRICE: Aye. When it a-comes to work one's
boy's a boy, two boys be half a boy, and three
boys be no boy at all.

*(Quiet laughter. They are enjoying the rest and
their pipes)*

PUMPKIN: Look at that.
OLD DAVID: Uh?
PUMPKIN: Yellowhammer — after them crumbs.
BOAMER: It's a good cage bird is a yellowhammer.

(Silence. Then OLD DAVID gets up)

OLD DAVID: Well — I be going up the hedge to
relieve myself.
BISHIE: You know what they say, Master Tuffrey
— eat well, work well, sleep well and shit well once
a day.

*(Appreciative laughter. OLD DAVID ambles
away. There is a ruminative silence)*

BISHIE: *(singing)* Adam catched Eve by the fur
    below
And that's the oldest catch we know.
PUMPKIN: That it be, Bishie.
BISHIE: I wonder why it don't say drink well once a
day. Or, come to that, you-know-what well once a
day, eh Pumpkin?
PUMPKIN: That's cause not even a well known old
ram like Mr Price here could do that, not 'im, not
with them bellies swelled out here with children.
BISHIE: Aye. 'Tis more like rolling off than rolling
on ain't it?

(Smothered laughter. Silence)

BISHIE: Here what 'tis said the Rector asked Mrs
Spicer?
OLD STUT: Sh-Sh-shame on you, B-Bishie.
PUMPKIN: Oh shut you up, Old Stut.
BISHIE: Rector says "Morning there Mrs Spicer
my good woman. Why be you wearing them
trousers to go to your work afield? I thought you
didn't have no unmentionables."

(First laughter)

Mrs Spicer says "I don't know what you'm a-talking about I'm sure. I thought the only unmentionables in your ears was Mr Gladstone".

(Laughter)

PUMPKIN: How many unmentionables have you got, Master Price?
OLD PRICE: I've enough for one life time I can tell 'ee!
BISHIE: Well said, Master Price.
OLD PRICE: The brimstone's fair coming out of your young mouths this mornin'.
BOAMER: Aye. If you're not careful there'll be some woman comin' along the road.
PUMPKIN: Aye. Oh aye. 'Tis field talk when all's said and done.

(BISHIE does not really agree but he shuts up. A thoughtful silence.

SAM starts to sing)

> *SAM'S SONG*
>
> As I was going to the fair of Athy,
> I spied a girl's petticoat hung out to dry,
> I took off my trousers,
> And I hung them close by,
> To keep that girl's petticoat warm.
>
> The petticoat flapped,
> And it made a loud noise,
> It flounced and it fluttered,
> Lost feminine poise,
> And it wound round the legs of my old
>   corduroys,

Oh, trousers, I hope you're on form!

(Still silence, each in his own thoughts)

OLD PRICE: Aye. It were thirty year ago, when I faced the old bull at Fishponds.

(Short silence)

It were the year my brother James married that Candleford woman. By hem but she were near! She were that near she 'udn't give away enough to make a pair of leggings for a skylark.

(Quiet laughter)

PUMPKIN: What became of her, Master Price?
OLD PRICE: Dead, Pumpkin, lad. Stone dead.

(Silence)

BOAMER: What does your old watch say now, Master Price?

(OLD PRICE gets his watch out)

OLD PRICE: Half an hour on, Boamer.

(BOAMER stands to call his men back to work)

BOAMER: All my gang back here! Follow your King of the Mowers!

(The band starts to play the same HARVEST SONG. The gang reforms, mows a swathe and passes on . The music builds to a climax and stops)

(They pass through the wheatfield)

END OF ACT TWO

ACT THREE

Scene 1
Afternoon
A BIT OF A TELL

*The women and children have had their meagre
dinners. Now the women sit outdoors with their
babies or their sewing or a novelette.*

*EMMA and MRS PEVERILL sit quietly and
happily in the sun.*

*LAURA and EDMUND come up to their mother
and kiss her.*

EMMA: Where are you off to?
LAURA: Walking with Martha Beamish. Up the
turnpike.
EMMA: And Edmund?
EDMUND: Yes, mother.
EMMA: Mind you're back before the cooking
smoke goes up.
LAURA: Yes, mother.

*(LAURA and EDMUND go, passing as they do so
QUEENIE, who is returning home in her green
veil and sheepskin gloves and has the bees in a
straw skep)*

*MRS PEVERILL, who has been waiting the right
moment to start a conversation calls across to
EMMA)*

MRS PEVERILL: 'Tis a good read I have 'ere, Mrs
Timms. 'Tis one o' them where the lady loves a
gamekeeper. But if you ask me him's a duke in
disguise.

(EMMA smiles and nods. She too likes a good

story but she does not wish to talk about this one.
Then MRS PEVERILL speaks again)

MRS PEVERILL: Lord save us!
EMMA: What from?
MRS PEVERILL: Mrs Andrews coming round for a
gossip.

(MRS ANDREWS has no children still at home,
which is why she has the time and the loneliness to
be a gossip)

MRS ANDREWS: Afternoon, Mrs Peverill. After-
noon, Mrs Timms.
EMMA: Afternoon, Mrs Andrews, won't you sit
down?
MRS ANDREWS: No. Oh no, thank 'ee. I mustn't
stop a minute.
MRS PEVERILL: Think weather's a-goin' to hold?
MRS ANDREWS: It's not weather as worries me so
much as Mrs Beamish.
EMMA: Mrs Beamish?
MRS ANDREWS: But a day or two off her time and
not a stitch put into a rag yet.
EMMA: Oh Mrs Andrews, I'm sure she's plenty left
over from her last baby.
MRS ANDREWS: I been a-watching her clothes line.
Not a new bit o' sewing's come out there.
MRS PEVERILL: Well there's always the Rector's
daughter and the clothes box.
MRS ANDREWS: Oh aye: and a slut's work is never
done. And as for that young Jim Shaw — well,
you knows what I've allus said about *him*.

(Silence. MRS ANDREWS waits for a response.
EMMA won't give one and this inhibits MRS
PEVERILL. MRS ANDREWS has to continue)

I seen a well-dressed man knockin' at their door to
tell poor Mrs Shaw that young Jim's in trouble
over money. I knows it for a fac'.

(Silence)

EMMA: Are you sure you won't sit down, Mrs
Andrews?
MRS ANDREWS: I mustn't stop a minute, Mrs
Timms. Why here's Mistress Macey poor old soul.
They all be saying dreadful things about her
Twister.

*(QUEENIE sits on her wooden stool and works
the beads on her lace cushion)*

(Silence)

MRS ANDREWS: Have you seen that Polly Arless
home on her holiday from service? And that Mary
Mullins. If you ask me they looks in the family
way, both on 'em!
MRS PEVERILL: I'm sure they h'ain't, Mrs
Andrews.
MRS ANDREWS: I've sized 'em up, Mrs Peverill,
and I'll tell 'ee another thing — and this I do know
for a fac'. Young Teddy the Prince of Wales has
given one of his fancy women a necklace with
pearls, the size o' pigeons' eggs and the poor old
Queen, God bless her, with her crown on 'er head
and tears a-runnin' down her cheeks had to go
down on her bended knees and a-beg him to turn
the whole lot of saucy hussies out o' Windsor
Castle.
MRS PEVERILL: Ooh! I call that shameful. And did
him?
MRS ANDREWS: Did him what?
MRS PEVERILL: Did him turn 'em out?

MRS ANDREWS: He refused. I know it for a fac'. I mustn't stop a minute longer. I only come out to borrow a spoonful o' tea from Mrs Ashley.

(MRS ANDREWS goes on her way round the Rise)

MRS PEVERILL: Never sits down do she?
EMMA: Mrs Andrews? No. Standing gossips always stay longest.
MRS PEVERILL: It's her children havin' grown-up. The wooman's got no one to talk to. Still — I think she makes a bit of a change even when I do see lies coming out of her mouth like steam.

(EMMA smiles. Silence)

EMMA: How's your lace coming, Mrs Peverill?
MRS PEVERILL: Not like the old days, Mrs Timms. I only does it now to keep my hand in. They've killed 'um with they Nottingham machines. Them wer'the days — when I wer' a girl like your Laura, and we took a year's work to Banbury Fair. Them wer' the days Mrs Timms. Money to spend! I bought calico and linsey-wolsey and that chocolate print I still got a piece of on my old quilt, and pipes and packets o' shag for the men, and rag dolls and ginger-bread and snuff and tripe.
EMMA: Tripe?
MRS PEVERILL: Tripe. Only time in the year we had it. I'd heat 'un up wi' an onion an' a nice bit o' thickening. Oh, I could curl up my toes at a nice bit o' thickenin'. Then us had the elderberry wine, Mrs Timms. Them wer' the days!

(Silence. EMMA works at her sewing)

MRS PEVERILL: My wine were very good this year. I done a good lot o' coltsfoot and the parsnip were real strong. My man likes that.

(They sit quietly. Then MRS BLABY comes out of her cottage)

MRS PEVERILL: Afternoon, Mrs Blaby.
MRS BLABY: Mrs Peverill.
EMMA: Afternoon.
MRS BLABY: Afternoon, Mrs Timms. Well I must say I feels all the better for that. I locked my door and I washed up as far as possible and down as far as possible.
MRS PEVERILL: What about possible itself?
MRS BLABY: I heard that, Mrs Peverill, and I'd call it men's talk.

(MRS PEVERILL and MRS BLABY laugh. Then they look at EMMA, who has not laughed, but who feels that she must nevertheless respond to them.

Sound of skylark)

EMMA: I love this time of day.
MRS PEVERILL: Aye. It's a woman's one bit o'rest.

(Silence)

MRS BLABY: Remember when my Aggie was home on her holidays last year and the dress on her were sky blue wi' very wide sleeves?
MRS PEVERILL: That were the best dress come to the Rise last year.
MRS BLABY: She sent it in her parcel.
MRS PEVERILL: She never.
MRS BLABY: She did. I'll have to let 'un out o' course. But it be real dressy. I do love anything a bit dressy.
MRS PEVERILL: I'd call that summat to save for high days and holidays and bonfire nights.

MRS BLABY: She sent a hat an' all.
MRS PEVERILL: Never.
MRS BLABY: Very wide brim it has.
MRS PEVERILL: That's the fashion, ain't it? I'd not
be seen goin' to the privy in one of them chimney
pot hats.

(Smiles. Silence)

EMMA: How old's your Aggie now, Mrs Blaby?
MRS BLABY: Sixteen. But I told her — I allus tells
my gals — that if they goes gettin' themselves into
trouble they'll have to go to the workhouse for I
won't have 'em at home.
MRS PEVERILL: So I tells mine. I think it's why I've
had no trouble with 'em.

(Silence)

MRS BLABY: Emily's baby though. Ain't she a
beauty?
MRS PEVERILL: They allus do say that that sort of
child *is* the finest.
MRS BLABY: What I say is the wife ought to have
the first child and the husband the second then
there wouldn't ever be any more.

(Silence)

MRS PEVERILL: My, your complexion do look fine,
Mrs Timms.
EMMA: I wash my face in rainwater.
MRS BLABY: That's it then.

(Silence)

MRS PEVERILL: How about a cup o' tay?
MRS BLABY: Aye.

MRS PEVERILL: Cup o' tay, Mrs Timms?
EMMA: No thank you. I think I'll just go inside for a bit of a lie down.

(EMMA goes in)

MRS BLABY: She's a bit la di da that Mrs Timms.
MRS PEVERILL: Well, she's in with all them young married ones.
MRS BLABY: She's expecting again ain't she?
MRS PEVERILL: Aye.
MRS BLABY: Not that she falls out with nobody.
MRS PEVERILL: Can't afford to, can us, in a place as small as this 'un?
MRS BLABY: Come on. I'll ask Mrs Miller to have that cup o' tay with us.

Scene 2

LAURA, EDMUND, MARTHA, and the LADY BAND SINGER now come on singing and playing

THE OLD WOMAN FROM CUMBERLAND

CHORUS:
Here comes an old woman from Cumberland
With all her children in her hand
And please do you want a servant today?

EDMUND:
What can they do? What can they do?

CHORUS:
This can brew and this can bake
This can make a wedding cake
This can wear a gay gold ring
This can sit in the barn and sing

This can go to bed with a king
And this one can do everything.

EDMUND:
Oh I will have that one
Yes I will have that one

(EDMUND selects someone and they have a tug-of-war)

CHORUS:
Goodbye, Mother, goodbye.

(One side wins. They then play the game two more times, first with additional members of the company, and, for the final time, with members of the audience as well)
(There is then a crashing chord from the band)

EDMUND: We can't go down here.
LAURA: This is the way.
EDMUND: We can't go.
MARTHA: Why can't we?
EDMUND: 'Cause that's the witch elder.
LAURA: What?
EDMUND: There. By the brook.

(They look)

LAURA: So 'tis. 'Tis the witch elder.
MARTHA: We can walk past it.
LAURA: Are you sure?
MARTHA: Course I am. 'Tis only if the tree's cut that it bleeds human blood.
LAURA: Do you believe that?
MARTHA: No. I don't believe in the beast's pond, neither.
LAURA: I've seen it.
MARTHA: My father says there's no such pond.

EDMUND: Oh yes there is.
MARTHA: There isn't.
LAURA: There is. But Queenie says that no one living's seen the monster.
EDMUND: But people did see.
LAURA: Course they did.
EDMUND: It's as big as a bullock but slimy, like a newt.
MARTHA: I don't believe none of it.
EDMUND: If you don't believe, Martha, you cut the elder tree.
MARTHA: I — I ain't got no knife have I? So I can't cut it can I?
EDMUND: I'll find a stone.

(The band plays and sings)

"WITCH ELDER"

Get up get up my father cried
For the witch is in my bed
She's in my bed and in my head
And in the candle flame

(The Music continues)

MARTHA: How could she be in a tree?
LAURA: Because she was an old woman who lived in the Rise. Men and boys chased her with pitch-forks until she reached the brook. Well, witches can't cross running water so she turned herself into this elder tree. Next morning there was an old woman fetching water from the well and here was this tree that hadn't been there before standing by the brook.

(EDMUND has found a sharp stone)

EDMUND: Here's one. You could cut with this one.

(The band sings)

> Don't cut the tree my father cried
> For the witch is the leaves
> She's in the leaves and in the sheaves
> And in the cloudless sky . . .

(The music stops abruptly.

MARTHA must decide what to do)

MARTHA: What if the tree really bleeds? What if the witch comes out and runs after us?

(More music)

(The children run round the space then stop and look at GARIBALDI JACKET who is on the first level)

MARTHA: Please, mum — do you want a maid?
GARIBALDI: Yes. Do you want a place?
MARTHA: Yes, mum.
GARIBALDI: What's your name?
MARTHA: Martha Beamish, mum.
GARIBALDI: How old are you?
MARTHA: Twelve.
GARIBALDI: What can you do?

(MARTHA is not sure. She looks at LAURA. LAURA is not sure, either)

Can you do what you're told?
MARTHA: Yes, mum.
GARIBALDI: Well that sounds right. This isn't a hard place because although there are sixteen rooms only three or four of them are in use. Can you get up at six without being called?

MARTHA: Yes, mum.

GARIBALDI: There's the kitchen range to light and the flues to be swept once a week, the dining-room to be swept and dusted and the fire lit before breakfast. I'm down myself in time to prepare breakfast. No cooking's required, beyond preparing vegetables.

MARTHA: Yes, mum.

GARIBALDI: After breakfast you'll help me with the beds and turning out the rooms and paring the potatoes and so on; and after dinner there's plenty to do — washing-up, cleaning knives and boots and polishing silver.

MARTHA: Yes, mum.

GARIBALDI: There'll be more jobs in the evening of course but at nine o'clock you'll be free to go to bed — after placing hot water in my bedroom.

MARTHA: Yes, mum.

GARIBALDI: Then, as wages, I can offer you two pounds ten a year. It is not a great wage but you are very small and you'll have an easy place and a comfortable home. You won't feel lonely, will you?

MARTHA: No, mum.

GARIBALDI: Tell your mother I shall expect her to fit you out well. You will want caps and aprons. I like my maids to look neat. And tell her to let you bring plenty of changes, for we only wash once in six weeks. I have a woman to do it all up.

(LAURA looks at MARTHA because she remembers what MRS BEAMISH said. But MARTHA is bewildered)

MARTHA: Yes, mum.

GARIBALDI: Well I shall expect you next Monday then.

MARTHA: Yes, mum.

GARIBALDI: Good. Now. Are you all hungry?
MARTHA: Yes, mum.
EDMUND: Oh yes, mum.
GARIBALDI: Then let's see what there is in the
pantry.

*(As it must sound on an old church harmonium —
an impression of Victorian good works)*

END OF ACT THREE

ACT FOUR

Scene 1

Evening. Cheapjack

The CHEAPJACK has a cart of crockery and tinware and a rigged-up backcloth painted with icebergs and penguins and polar bears. He lights a naphtha flare and clashes his basins together like bells. People gather round him.

CHEAPJACK: Come buy! Come buy! Look at these bargains! Twenty one pieces of a tea service and not a flaw in any one of them! The Queen has its fellow in Buckingham Palace!
MRS PEVERILL: Mrs Timms! Mrs Timms! 'Tis a cheapjack!
CHEAPJACK: Look at this! Look! Twenty one pieces! And look at this! Just listen to the music of this chamber pot!

(He rings the pots with his knuckles)

Sweet music in the night! Sweet music!
MRS MILLER: Oh what forrard jokes!
CHEAPJACK: You don't like jokes, Missis? You don't like humourosity? I'll give you a song.

(He sings and the band plays)

CHEAPJACK'S SONG

There was a man in his garden walked
And cut his throat with a lump of chalk
His wife, she knew not what she did
She strangled herself with the saucepan lid

In and out the window
In and out the window
In and out the window
Until the break of day

There was a man and a fine young fellow
Who poisoned himself with an umbrella
Even Joey in his cot
Shot himself dead with a chamber pot

In and out the window
In and out the window
In and out the window
Until the break of day

When you hear this horrible tale
It makes your faces all turn pale
Your eyes go green, you're overcome
So tweedle tweedle tum.

*(The song is well liked. It launches the
CHEAPJACK into his patter)*

CHEAPJACK: Two bob! Only two bob for this
handsome set of jugs! Here's one for your beer
and one for your milk and another in case you
break one of the other two. Nobody's willing to
speculate?

*(Cue for Harvest Song II as the men return from
the fields and gather round the cart)*

HARVEST SONG II

Our oats they're hoed
And our barley's reaped
Our hay it is mowed
And our hovels heaped.

Come boys come, Come boys come,
And merrily roar out harvest home.
Harvest home, harvest home,
We'll merrily roar out harvest home.

We've cheated the parson
We'll cheat him again,
Why should the old bugger
Have one in ten?

One in ten, one in ten,
Why should the old bugger have one in ten?
Harvest home, harvest home,
We'll merrily roar out harvest home.

Then what about this 'ere set of trays straight
from Japan and the peonies hand-painted? Or this
lot of basins, exact replicas of the one the Princess
of Wales supped her gruel from when Prince
George was born. Why, damme, they cost me
more'n two bob! I could get twice the two bob I'm
asking here, in Banbury tomorrow. But I'll give
'em to you — for at two bob you can't call it
selling — because I like your faces and my load's
so heavy me horses refused to pull it. Alarming
bargains! Tremendous sacrifices! Come buy!
Come buy!

Threepence for a large pudding basin! A dozen
tumblers and a ball of string! Sixpence for a tin
saucepan! Wooden spoons! A penny nutmeg
grater! Come buy! Come buy!

(The music comes closer. The returning men are singing almost under their breaths. Gradually, wearily, they gather round to watch the CHEAPJACK)

Never let it be said that this place — what's it called?
LAURA: Lark Rise.
CHEAPJACK: Lark Rise. Never let it be said that Lark Rise is the poverty-strickenest place on God's earth! Here! Good dinner plates for you! Every one a left-over from a first-class service. Buy one of these and you'll have the satisfaction of knowing that you're eating off the same ware as Lords and Dukes! Only three half-pence each! Who'll buy? Who'll buy?

(One or two women buy)

That's better! That's more like the old England! Now look at these you men home from work. Look at this tea service. You just look at the light through it.

(He hands out pieces of crockery)

And you madam. And you, sir. Ain't it lovely china, thin as an eggshell, practically transparent and with every one of them roses handpainted with a brush. You can't let a set like that go out of the place now can you? I can see all your mouths a-watering. All run home and bring out them stockings from under your mattresses and the first one to get back shall have it for twelve bob!

(Silence. Nobody moves)

PUMPKIN: Twelve bob! By hem! We ain't got twelve pence.

(There is a slightly ashamed laughter from the crowd)

MRS PEVERILL: I don't like it. It ain't good to look poor as well as bein' poor.
CHEAPJACK: Oh come on then. It *is* poverty-stricken. Hand them pieces back. I won't shame you.

(People hand the pieces back. At the same time they do *feel ashamed.*

Then JOHN PRICE the returned soldier speaks up)

PRICE: How much did you say, mister? Twelve bob? I'll give you ten.
PUMPKIN: Wert up, John lad! No flinchin'!
PRICE: I'll give you ten bob.
CHEAPJACK: Can't be done, matey. Cost me more nor that. But look see. I tell you what I will do. You give me eleven and six and I'll throw in this handsome silver gilt vase for your mantelpiece.
PRICE: Done!

(Music again. Applause. The hamlet's good name is saved. People help JOHN PRICE to carry off his tea-service)

Scene 2

Tea

EMMA: You deserve a darn good bommicking, that's what you deserve.
LAURA: No we don't.
EMMA: Yes you do. You told me you were going

up the turnpike, but you went with Martha to see about her petty place, didn't you?

LAURA: Yes.

EMMA: Yes, well Mrs Beamish couldn't go but you did and that was very thoughtful, but telling me a lie was sinful. You can lock up from a thief but you can't from a liar. Well, what have you got to say for yourself?

EDMUND: It was a waste of time.

EMMA: What?

EDMUND: Martha forgot to ask for her wages in advance, so her mother won't let her go. And anyway, they say it's a haunted house.

EMMA: Edmund, if you aren't a better boy, old Oliver Cromwell will have you.

(EDMUND does not seem very hungry)

EMMA: Edmund. Eat up.

(No response)

Edmund.

EDMUND: Please, mother, I'm not very hungry.

EMMA: You walked far enough.

EDMUND: The lady at the big house gave us roast beef.

EMMA: Did she now?

EDMUND: I had four helpings.

EMMA: Then you can leave that alone and put it on your father's plate.

(EDMUND puts his knife and fork together. EMMA and LAURA finish their meal in silence. EMMA looks at the children. LAURA and EDMUND put their hands together)

LAURA: Thank God for my good tea. Thank father and mother. Amen.

EDMUND: Amen.
EMMA: Amen.

(EMMA gets up and starts to bustle)

Now. We'll keep your father's food warm in the pot so the pig can't have the cooking water yet; but what you can do is help me clear these plates. Come on.

(EMMA looks back at LAURA and EDMUND. They are both sitting very glumly)

Laura. Edmund. What's the matter?

(LAURA and EDMUND look at each other. Then LAURA speaks)

LAURA: Mother. We're sorry if we told lies. Aren't we?
EDMUND: Yes.
LAURA: It's just that we didn't think you'd let us go.
EMMA: Oh I'd have let you go, Laura. Or I hope I would. I understand that Old Sally wants you to help her.
LAURA: Yes.
EMMA: Well, I'm proud of you — but I don't want you to tell me any of Sally's business. That *wouldn't* be right. Understand?
LAURA: Yes.
EMMA: That's all right then. I tell you what. Help clear these plates and then have a bit of a read and go to bed with a peppermint each. How's that?
LAURA: Oh! Can we!

(EMMA and LAURA clear. EDMUND sits thinking)

EDMUND: Mother. Are there any witches now?
EMMA: No. They seem to have all died out. But when I was your age there were plenty of old people who'd known one. Of course we know there were *witches* because we read about them in the Bible.

(LAURA and EDMUND exchange a glance)

What book are *you* reading now, Laura?
LAURA: "Gulliver's Travels".
EMMA: Oh, that was given me by the Reverend Mr Johnstone, when I was a nursemaid to his children.
LAURA: Mother, shall we put these flowers on the table for when father sits down?
EMMA: That's a *very* good idea, Laura.

(LAURA moves the jar of flowers from the window sill to the table, where Albert's place awaits him)

LAURA: Mother, is it true you nearly didn't marry father?
EMMA: Well, I nearly went to Australia.
EDMUND: Why didn't you?
EMMA: I would have gone but somebody told me about the snakes there and I said "I won't go, for I can't abide the horrid creatures."
LAURA: Did you know father already?
EMMA: No. There was a stonemason needed to work on the church and as you know your father was sent from Oxford.
EDMUND: When you met him and got married and lived happy ever after in this house.
EMMA: Yes.
LAURA: He is late again isn't he?
EDMUND: He's here, it's him. It's father!

EMMA: If you can see when he comes in that he's cross don't ask him questions.

(EDMUND glances out into the dusk)

(The door opens and ALBERT stands there. He is belligerently drunk)

EMMA: Albert. You're late, my dear.
ALBERT: No I'm not.
EMMA: We've had our tea. Haven't we children?
ALBERT: Good. Very good. That means there's room at the table for my friend.
EMMA: Your friend? What friend?
ALBERT: Come on, friend. Enter, friend.

(A TRAMP comes uneasily in. He is a dirty unshaven man in rags and a battered bowler)

TRAMP: Good evening. God bless you, mum. Good evening.
EMMA: Albert. He's a tramp.
TRAMP: That's right.
ALBERT: I found him in a ditch. I heard a noise and looked down and there he was.
EMMA: You go upstairs, children. You can finish your reading in bed, Laura. Then I'll come up to say Gentle Jesus.

(LAURA and EDMUND go upstairs.)

ALBERT: Come on, brother. Sit down.
EMMA: Albert!
ALBERT: Sit yourself down. There's a place laid.
TRAMP: Thank you. Thank you, brother.
EMMA: This is no brother of mine.
ALBERT: Gentle Jesus meek and mild, look upon this little child — but don't look upon this man in the ditch is that it?

EMMA: Albert — he smells.
TRAMP: I had just such an house as you'n, mum.
It burned down in a flood.

(EMMA gives him half a loaf)

EMMA: Yes well you take this here.
TRAMP: Thank you, mum. Thank you.
EMMA: And now you've got it, go! Go on!
Go! . . .
TRAMP: Thank you, mum! God bless you! God
bless you.

(The TRAMP goes)

EMMA: I can't have them in the house, Albert. I
can't. When in Rome I must do as the Romans do.
ALBERT: This isn't Rome. It's Lark Rise. The spot
God made with left-overs when he'd finished
creating the rest of the earth.

(ALBERT sits down. Silence. EMMA gets his tea)

I was born on the very day — the very day — of
the Battle of Alma.
EMMA: I know. I know you were.
ALBERT: We were fighting the Russians. Hard and
cruel they were, and thought that might was right,
but found themselves mistaken. They could not
make slaves of a free people.

(Silence)

EMMA: Laura and me put the flowers for you.

*(ALBERT is moved. He wants very much to
communicate with her and to live in a way that
enables him to express his ideals)*

ALBERT: They're none of them — not one of them — as beautiful as you.

(EMMA sits. Silence. They are both moved. Then EMMA decides that since nothing can be changed it is best to be normal and to tell the hamlet news of the day)

EMMA: They took poor Mr Sharman away this morning and, what d'you think, my father managed to walk round.
ALBERT: Did you see old Sharman go?
EMMA: He took it very hard.
ALBERT: Did they leave him his dignity?
EMMA: No.

(Silence)

ALBERT: How are the children? What's Laura's book?
EMMA: "Gulliver's Travels".
ALBERT: Good. Good. *(He lifts his head so that LAURA upstairs can hear him shout)* Good girl, Laura!

(ALBERT and EMMA stare at each other)

How are you, my dear? How do you feel?
EMMA: I feel very well, Albert, considering I'm in my fourth month.

(Silence. EMMA gets up and looks out of the window)

EMMA: There's young Fisher saying goodbye to his Polly.

(FISHER and POLLY are standing in the doorway of her mother's cottage)

FISHER: Don't 'ee fret, Polly. You'll go back to your place tomorrow and in another twelve month you'll be back here bursting wi' London pride and a twelve month after that we'll be married.

(POLLY weeps a little. FISHER holds her.

EMMA turns away from the window)

EMMA: How about you, Albert? How was your work? Are you as tired as you look?
ALBERT: Me? I'm as happy as a lark. Come Michaelmas we'll give notice here and move over to Candleford.

(Music)

Scene 3
The Wagon and Horses

LANDLORD: The first day of the harvest went well then?
PUMPKIN: Went well? We dragged us guts out.
BISHIE: Good old Boamer lad.
LANDLORD: So they did you proud, Boamer.
BOAMER: They did. That they did, Landlord. And will tomorrow, until the work be done with no flinching.

(OLD DAVID makes his entrance)

BISHIE: Here be the oldest inhabitant still workin' and drinkin'!
OLD PRICE: Evening David.
OLD DAVID: Evening.
PUMPKIN: I thought you might have brung out your secret savings, Master Tuffrey, and bought that tea service off the Cheapjack.

BISHIE: If you had you could have been like young Mrs Shaw what was in very la di da service.
OLD PRICE: What about Mrs Shaw?
BISHIE: Ties a blue bow round the handle of her chamber pot.

(Laughter)

OLD DAVID: It's when I hear you boys a-talking that I understands why the old rector preaches agin this place. What did he call it?
BISHIE: A den of iniquity.
PUMPKIN: That be it!
OLD PRICE: We can't afford more than one half pint of a night and he calls it a den of iniquity!

(Laughter)

BISHIE: Ask me, 'tis a great pity he can't come and see what it's like for his own self.
OLD PRICE: Pity he can't mind his own business.

(Focus switches on the first level where EMMA prays with the children)

EMMA AND CHILDREN:
   Gentle Jesus, meek and mild,
   Look upon this little child.
   Pity my simplicity,
   And suffer me to come to thee.
OLD DAVID: Well, 'tis his business, come to think on't. The man's mind paid to preach and he's got to find summat to preach against, stands to reason.

(Back in the pub, ALBERT makes his entrance)

BISHIE: Evening, Mr Timms.

ALBERT: Evening.

OLD DAVID: Evening.

OLD PRICE: We was just a-talking about the old rector.

ALBERT: Don't the women say that his chief virtue is that when he visits them at home he never talks about religion?

BISHIE: Can't leave much else, can it?

OLD DAVID: Him's a gentleman born, though.

OLD PRICE: He is. He's no counter-jumper.

ALBERT: He's no right to talk politics from the pulpit — which he does, and has done ever since they gave householders the vote.

PUMPKIN: Well spoke, Mr Timms. I worked away in Northampton and I be radical.

LANDLORD: I'm a true blue, Pumpkin, so mind your sentiments.

(Women outside are listening)

MRS PEVERILL: Here it be! Politics! Now you listen!

PUMPKIN: Joseph Arch is my sentiments, Landlord. Joseph Arch is the man for the farm labourer and I'm proud to have a-shook of his hand.

LANDLORD: If I was in Downing Street I'd not give house room to Joseph Arch nor his Trades Union.

BISHIE: What does it matter who's in Downing Street? Whoever 'tis they won't give us nothin', and they can't take nothing away from us, for you can't get blood out of a stone.

PUMPKIN: That's not you talking is it, Bishie?

BOAMER: Oh he's up on the roof one minute and down the well the next.

BISHIE: What's having the vote done for us? Tell me that?

OLD DAVID: First time I had a vote Squire

Bracewell drove me in his carriage. But I voted
Liberal! He! He!

BOAMER: I should hope you did, father.

OLD DAVID: They took the poor old hoss to the
water but he didn't drink out of their trough! Not
he!

ALBERT: I call that a bit low down, to roll up in
anybody's carriage to vote against them.

OLD DAVID: Low down? It were rainin'.

OLD PRICE: Ask me David we gets ten bob a week
and we earns every penny of it; but we doesn't
earn no more; we takes hemmed good care o' that!

(Laughter)

ALBERT: What does that show, Master Price?

OLD PRICE: What do it show? It shows us knows us
own mind. We don't live in no threepence a week
tied house 'cause it stands to reason that them as
does allus got to do just what they be told or out
they goes.

OLD DAVID: Neck and crop.

OLD PRICE: Bag and baggage. But us can't be told
'cause us pay a shillin' a week to live in the Rise.

ALBERT: That didn't save old Sharman did it?

OLD PRICE: It saved him afore he got feeble!

(The women outside have been eagerly following)

MRS PEVERILL: There! See? The old cocks don't
like it when the young cocks start to crow.

LANDLORD: Say as you will it's no good you chaps
thinking you're goin' against the gentry.

MRS BLABY: Just what I says! If the men have to
vote why don't they vote Tory and keep in with
the gentry?

MRS PEVERILL: You don't never hear of Liberals
giving the poor a bit o' coal or a blanket at
Christmas do you?

MRS BLABY: O' course not. O' course we don't.
LANDLORD: They've got the land and they've got
the money *and* they'll keep it. Where'd *you* be
without them to give you work and pay your
wages, I'd like to know.

*(ALBERT decides that the moment to speak has
come)*

ALBERT: Where we'd be Landlord, is where we are
now — all of us a-voting for Mr Gladstone who
can change things and make 'em better.

(The men heartily agree, even the old ones)

OLD DAVID: Well, I never thought I'd agree that
much with 'ee, Mr Timms.
BOAMER: Come on, lads. "People's William".

(They all burst into the song)

"THE PEOPLE'S WILLIAM"

God bless the people's William
Long may he lead the van
Of Liberty and freedom
God bless the Grand Old Man
Hip Hip Hooray!

(The men heartily applaud themselves.

The LANDLORD decides to change the subject)

LANDLORD: How's about a bit of a song from you,
Algy? Just to oblige?

*(ALGY is tall, thin and getting old, a weedy
stooping creature with watery blue eyes and long*

ginger side-whiskers. His voice is high and a bit
cracked but there is something about him of both
a military bearing and a man of culture)

ALGY: Oh Bai Jove, I say, Landlord, I mean dash
it all, Bai Jove . . .
ALBERT: I hear they've put him on half pay.
LANDLORD: Well: what can he do except work
with the women?
PUMPKIN: Come on, Algy. Wert up!
ALGY: When I . . . when I was in the Grenadier
Guards . . .
BOAMER: Where does he come from? That's what
I'd like to know.
OLD PRICE: Knocked at the door of an house
didn't he?
OLD DAVID: Twenty year ago.
OLD PRICE: At midnight. In a thunderstorm.
PUMPKIN: Remember what he did when the
German band came?
BISHIE: German Band, Algy.
ALGY: Bai Jove. What?
PUMPKIN: German Band's a-comin'!

(The band oomph-oompahs like the German band
that visits the hamlet once a year.

ALGY sticks his fingers in his ears and howls.
Then the music stops. ALGY looks bewildered)

ALBERT: Joking, Algy. Only joking.
ALGY: Bai Jove . . .
BISHIE: What about that song then?
ALGY: To oblige, what? Same as usual? Ready!
Steady! Go!

(ALGY sings)

HAVE YOU EVER BEEN IN THE PENNINSULA?

Have you ever been in the Penninsula?
If not I advise you to stay where you haw
For should you adore a
Sweet Spanish senor-ah
She may prove what some might call sin-gu-lah!

(The men clap politely while ALGY returns to his seat. COCKIE and MASTER PRIDHAM enter the pub)

BOAMER: Evening Cockie.
BISHIE: Master Pridham.

(The focus switches to the first level where LAURA and EDMUND are being put to bed by EMMA)

LAURA: Mother . . .
EMMA: Shhhh . . . Go back to sleep.
LAURA: Where's father?
EMMA: He's just walked out a while.
LAURA: Will you walk out?
EMMA: I might go and sit at the door with Queenie.
LAURA: Tell me a story.
EMMA: No, Laura. Edmund's asleep.
LAURA: Something out of your own head.
EMMA: Well, first you lie down again.
Once upon a time there was a little girl and when she wasn't out for mushrooms she was out for berries, on a heath just like Hardwick Heath, where we went blackberrying you know, and when she looked down under one bush she saw a little wooden door in the ground. She opened the door and there was some steps and she went down the

steps and what d'you think? They led to an under-
ground palace where everything was blue and
silver. Silver tables and silver chairs and silver
plates to eat off and all the cushions and curtains
were made of pale blue satin.

(The focus returns to the Pub)

LANDLORD: Come on, Chad. Do your bit. Paid on
in ale!

*(CHAD GUBBINS who is a morris dancer gets up
and does a dance. He uses BISHIE's hat as a
marker and at the end of the dance he jumps on it
and then returns it to BISHIE amid applause from
the men)*

PUMPKIN: What's old Master Price up to in his
corner over there? Ain't heard him strike up
tonight.
BISHIE: He only knows his old "Outlandish
Knight".
DOAMER: Poor old feller be eighty three. Let 'un
sing while he can.

(OLD PRICE rises and announces)

OUTLANDISH KNIGHT

OLD PRICE:
An outlandish knight from the Northlands
     came,
And he came a-wooing of me.

MRS PEVERILL: They'll soon be out now. There's
poor old Dave a-singing of his "Outlandish
Knight".

OLD PRICE:
And he told me he'd take me up to the
  Northlands,
And there he would marry me.

Go fetch me some of your father's gold,
And some of your mother's tea,
And the two finest horses from your father's
  stables,
Where there stand thirty and three.

He's mounted him up on his milk white steed,
She's rode on the dapple grey,
And they rode till they came to the broad sea-
  shore,
Three hours before it was day.

Light down, light down from your horse he
  cries,
And deliver it over to me,
For six pretty maids I have drowned here,
And the seventh one you'll surely be.

Take off, take off your silken gown,
And deliver it unto me,
For I think it's not fitting so costly a robe,
Should all rot away in the sea.

Light down, light down off your horse she
  cries,
And turn your back unto me,
I think it's not fitting a fine gentleman,
A naked lady should see.

He's lighted him down from his lily white steed,
And turned his back to she,
And she's catched him round his middle so
  small,
And tumbled him into the sea.

LANDLORD: Come on, Master Pridham, wert up!
Let's be having of my favourite — "Pratty
Flowers".

(MASTER PRIDHAM and the men sing)

ABROAD FOR PLEASURE

PRIDHAM:
Abroad for pleasure as I was a-walking
Twas on a summer, summer calm and clear.
ALL:
Abroad for pleasure as I was a-walking,
Twas on a summer, summer calm and clear.

PRIDHAM:
There I beheld the most beautiful damsel,
Lamenting for her shepherd swain.
ALL:
There I beheld the most beautiful damsel,
Lamenting for her shepherd swain,
Lamenting for her shepherd swain.

PRIDHAM:
Wilt thou go fight the French and Spaniards,
Wilt thou leave me thus my dear.
ALL:
Wilt thou go fight the French and Spaniards,
Wilt thou leave me thus my dear,
Wilt thou leave me thus my dear.

PRIDHAM:
No more to yon green banks will I take me,
With pleasure for to rest myself and view the
    lambs.
ALL:
No more to yon green banks will I take me,
With pleasure for to rest myself and view the
    lambs.

PRIDHAM:
But I will take me to yon green gardens,
Where the pratty flowers grow.
ALL:
But I will take me to yon green gardens,
Where the pratty flowers grow,
Where the pratty, pratty flowers grow.

(Applause as the song ends and then it is closing time)

LANDLORD: Well, that be it for another night, men.
OLD PRICE: Aye. That it is.

(The men begin to return their mugs and leave)

LANDLORD: You'll be leading them again tomorrow, Boamer.
BOAMER: That I will, for I'm the King of the Mowers.
PUMPKIN: Goodnight, Master Price.
OLD PRICE: Goodnight, Pumpkin.
ALGY: Bai Jove . . . What?
BISHIE: Don't you be forgetting your bedtime cup of soapsuds, Master Price.
OLD PRICE: Them cleans the outers, Bishie, so it stands to reason they clean the innards too.

(They have all left now except ALBERT and BOAMER who stand and shake hands)

ALBERT: Well. Goodnight, Boamer. Soon be harvest home.
BOAMER: Aye. It will. Soon be the old Queen's Jubilee an' all.

(The band now plays the hymn tune as the actors reset the benches for Church)

Scene 4

Memorial

The actors process into Church and the RECTOR goes up to the first level. They then stand and sing

THE DAY THOU GAVEST LORD IS ENDED

The day thou gavest Lord, is ended,
The darkness falls at thy behest;
To thee our morning hymns ascended,
Thy praise shall sanctify our rest.

(During the second verse LAURA and EDMUND walk to the back of the church)

So be it Lord, thy throne shall never,
Like earth's proud empires, pass away;
Thy kingdom stands, and grows for ever,
Till all thy creatures own thy sway.

LAURA: After the Jubilee, nothing ever seemed quite the same. The old rector died and the farmer retired and machines put people out of work. Early in the Nineties some measure of relief came, for then the weekly wage was raised to fifteen shillings; but rising prices and new requirements soon absorbed this rise, and it took a world war to obtain anything like a living wage.

(The band quietly plays)

THE BATTLE OF THE SOMME

RECTOR: To the Glory of God in memory of those from this parish whose lives have been given in defence of their country and in the cause of right and justice in the Great War 1914-1918 A.D. J. Blaby, W. Blaby, E. A. V. Blencowe, A. D. Cross, H. Farrer, S. Gaskin, H. Harris, E. Peverill, W. Peverill, E. Timms.

EDMUND: E. Timms? That's me!

LAURA: Hush, Edmund!

RECTOR: Their name liveth for evermore.

(The band reprise "BATTLE OF THE SOMME" as the actors line up for the final photo pose. They disperse with the music and this is the end of the play itself.

But then the leader of the band calls for a "Grand Circle Dance" and the cast form up and do the dance. Then members of the audience are invited to join in, and the whole process is repeated.

Finally the actors sit down with their partners as the lady in the band sings)

BONNY LABOURING BOY

As I roved out one May morning all in the
    blooming spring,
I overheard a maid complain and grievous did
    she sing,
How cruel were her parents, they did her so
    annoy,
And would not let her marry with her Bonny
    Labouring Boy.

Now Jonny was my true love's name as you
    may plainly see,
And my father he employed him his labouring
    boy to be,

To sow the seed and reap the hay all on my
    father's land,
And soon I fell in love with him as you may
    understand.

His hair is like the raven's wing, his eyes are
    black as jet,
His face it is the finest that ever I've seen yet,
He's manly, neat and handsome, his cheeks are
    like the snow,
And in spite of both my parents, with Jonny I
    shall go.

So fill your glasses to the brim, let the toast go
    merrily round,
Here's a health to every labouring man who
    ploughs and sows the ground,
And when his work is over, it's home he'll
    speed with joy,
And happy is the girl who weds her Bonny
    Labouring Boy.

BAND LEADER. Thank you and GOOD NIGHT,

MEMOIR

by
John Murrell

MEMOIR

In an earlier version, this play was first presented
at the Guelph Spring Festival of the Arts, Ontario,
Canada, on 2 May 1977, with Siobhán McKenna
as Sarah Bernhardt and Gerard Parkes as Pitou. It
was directed by Eric Salmon and designed by
Bruce Koenig, with costumes by Mary Kerr.
Special music was composed by Lucio Agostini.

Quest Publications staged the play at the
Ambassadors Theatre, London, on 11 January
1978, with the following cast:

SARAH BERNHARDT	*Siobhán McKenna*
GEORGES PITOU	*Niall Buggy*

Directed by William Chappell
Set designed by Mervyn Rowe
Lighting by Leslie Scott

Miss McKenna also appeared in the play at the
Olympia Theatre, Dublin.

CHARACTERS

Sarah Bernhardt, an actress
Georges Pitou, her secretary

AUTHOR'S NOTE

In this play I have consciously departed from history in one major way. I have kept Pitou in Bernhardt's service longer than she did herself. It is doubtful whether he was still with her during her last summer, although he did for many years keep notes for a second volume of her memoirs, which she never finished.

All translations in the script are my own.

The action takes place on the island of Belle-Ile-en-Mer, off the coast of Brittany.

ACT I
Late afternoon, summer, 1922

ACT II
Just before dawn the following day

ACT ONE

Les Poulains, Sarah Bernhardt's sprawling estate on the north point of the island of Belle-Ile-en-Mer. The terrace of the Penhoët manor house on a late afternoon in the summer of 1922.

The terrace is paved with flagstones, surrounded by tamarisks, pines, and a stone balustrade, and partially covered by a rough wooden roof. There are several outdoor and indoor type chairs, a bench draped with rugs and furs, a table with a clutter of paper, pens, pencils, and so on, and a small liquor cabinet. A piano has been rolled out at one end of the terrace.

The manor house, in the background, is enormous, dark, with many windows.

At one side, a steep stairway leads down to the sea, which can be heard occasionally throughout the play.

Sarah is asleep, propped up with cushions in a chair. The sea is heard very faintly. The red and amber of a setting sun spread across the terrace. Sarah is seventy-seven years old. Nearly eight years ago her right leg was amputated above the knee. The variety and amount of her movement are not precisely indicated in this script. When, where, and how she moves — with the aid of a cane and an artificial limb, in a wheelchair, or frequently supporting herself on convenient pieces of furniture — these are questions for the individual actress of the role and her director. All possible means of conveyance were attempted by Bernhardt at some point in her later life. She remains fiercely independent in spirit and she hates to appear foolish.

MUSIC: a rising phrase of sustained notes on a solo woodwind.

Sarah wakes. She looks out at the sun, which is

still very bright, and frowns. She glances around,
realizes she is alone. She turns and calls toward the
house:

SARAH: Pitou! *(Pause.)* Pitou! . . . Where is he?
PITOU!

(After a moment her secretary, Georges Pitou,
enters from the house. He is considerably younger
than Sarah, but with a balding, monastic appear-
ance and a fatigued manner, in contrast to her
constant vigour. His jacket and trousers have a
patina of grime. His cravat is clumsily tied and his
fingers are black with ancient ink. He has been
with Sarah a long time and sometimes treats her in
the manner of a husband of twenty years or
more.)

PITOU: Oh, here you are, Madame!
SARAH: And here *you* are. At last.
PITOU: Who brought you out here, I'd like to
know? That new fellow? Henri?
SARAH: This afternoon sun is like a fist, Pitou.
There's not a breath of air. Look at the sea. White
and silent as a punished child. Fetch my parasol.
PITOU: Yes, Madame. *(He starts to go, then turns*
back.) Or probably you'd rather be taken inside?
It's getting late and Dr Marot says a woman in
your condition must be careful not to —
SARAH: None of your nonsense! My parasol!
PITOU: At once.

(He exits into the house. Sarah sits up, brushes the
hair from her eyes, winces slightly, bites her lip.

MUSIC: as before, a sustained woodwind phrase,
rising.)

SARAH: I ought to accomplish something. *(Pause.)*
It's uncommonly hot. I'm tired. *(Pause.)* Yes. The
sun. Engaged in the long process of burning
herself to a cinder. So I'm told. Well — she won't
be easy to replace!

*(Pitou returns with a piece of embroidery, which
he brings to Sarah.)*

SARAH: What's this?
PITOU: Your sewing, Madame.
SARAH: That's not what I asked for!
PITOU: No?
SARAH: Parasol! My *parasol!* I'm dehydrating,
Pitou, drying out like an old —
PITOU: You have a fever!
SARAH: No! The sun!
PITOU: How did Madame get out here, with her
fever? Dr Marot recommended —
SARAH: *I've never had a fever in my life!*
PITOU: It starts with a slight fever, followed by
shortness of breath, bleeding at the mouth,
delirium, hysteria —!
SARAH: Pitou!
PITOU: And "Pitou!" you'll say, "Pitou, why
didn't you warn me? Why did you allow me to sit
out in the sun until —"
SARAH: *Pitou! (Pause.)* My parasol.
PITOU: At once.

(He starts out.)

SARAH: And bring the gramophone! Some music
might jog me back into life.
PITOU: The gramophone? Out here?
SARAH: Why not?
PITOU: The salt air. It corrodes the little cylinders,

the little cogs, the little wheels —

(She clinches her teeth, glares at him.)

PITOU: And music, Madame? Before supper? It's common medical knowledge that music irritates the digestive tract. My mother used to say, "The stomach and the ears are sympathetic organs and should not be —"
SARAH: *(Thundering)* THE GRAMOPHONE!
PITOU: At once!

(He exits into the house.)

SARAH: I promised to buy that fool a hairpiece — if, for just one day, he wouldn't torture me with his babbling — and his mother's medical opinions! But I know in my heart he'll go to his grave bald as an egg! *(Pause.)* Yes. The sun. *(Pause.)* I should have asked him to bring the notes. I'll work this afternoon. That'll surprise Maurice. He will suppose I just lay here all afternoon...like an old... lizard. Like some old lizard under the sun's fist. *(She smiles suddenly.)* My God, that's brilliant! Take this down, Pitou! *(She looks around, realizes he is not there.)* Pitou! Where is he?

(Pitou returns with the gramophone under one arm, an album of records under the other.)

SARAH: Ah, Pitou! Take this down exactly! "To the world at large, I had become an old lizard, lying under —"
PITOU: Where does Madame wish me to —?
SARAH: Shh!
PITOU: On the piano?

(He staggers to the piano, puts down the gramophone and records.)

SARAH: "I had become an old — *dehydrated* lizard lying under —" Pitou! Aren't you taking this down?

PITOU: No, Madame.

SARAH: Why not?

PITOU: I'm not — I can't — I don't know what we're doing, Madame! *(To himself) I never* know anymore.

SARAH: Where's my parasol?

PITOU: Madame?

SARAH: I distinctly asked for my *parasol!*

PITOU: You distinctly asked for the *gramophone!*

SARAH: *And* my parasol!

PITOU: No, I don't remember anything about —

SARAH: Wait!

(She grabs a scrap of paper from the table, scribbles on it with a pen. Pitou crosses, looks over her shoulder.)

SARAH: Look! I have *written* "P—A—R—A" —

PITOU: I can read, Madame.

SARAH: Then fetch! No! Take this with you!

(She thrusts the scrap of paper into his hand. He sighs and starts out.)

SARAH: And bring the notes, too!

PITOU: The notes?

SARAH: The blue folder with the gillyflowers. You know the one.

PITOU: Out here?

SARAH: Yes. *And* the parasol. *And* the notes in the blue folder.

PITOU: We're going to work on the Memoir?

SARAH: Yes.

PITOU: Then we won't need the gramophone.

(He starts toward the piano.)

SARAH: Leave it, Pitou! Go away!

(He starts out.)

SARAH: Pitou . . .?
PITOU: Hmm?
SARAH: Where are you going?
PITOU: Inside, Madame.
SARAH: Why?
PITOU: You distinctly told me: "Pitou, go away!" you said.
SARAH: To fetch something, wasn't it?
PITOU: *(After a moment's thought)* The blue folder? Our notes for Volume Two of the Memoir?
SARAH: And . . .?
PITOU: Madame?
SARAH: *And?*

(Pause.)

PITOU: The blue folder. With the gillyflowers.
SARAH: What's that in your hand, Pitou? Your *left* hand!
PITOU: *(He looks at it.)* Scrap of paper, Madame.
SARAH: *What's written on the paper, Pitou?!*

(Pause. He reads.)

PITOU: *(Grimacing)* Yes. All right. But I fail to see how a *parasol* can bring Madame relief from what is obviously an advanced case of dyspepsia, and nervous *fever!*

(He crams the paper into his pocket and exits into the house, talking to himself.)

PITOU: Better for all concerned if she would

consent to be removed to the cool and comfort of
her rooms. A little organization, that's all I ask!
I'm not a common servant, after all, to be sum-
moned and sent and made to suffer the tortures of
the damned at Madame's slightest whim . . .!

*(His voice fades. Pause. Sarah puts one hand on
her side, winces. A worried look passes across her
face. MUSIC: the rising woodwind phrase.)*

SARAH: Yes. Some music. *(She goes to the piano.)*
A melody by Mozart or Messager . . . to sting the
memory awake.

*(She takes the records, sorts through them, tossing
several aside. They clatter noisily across the piano
top.)*

SARAH: Caruso? Scotti? Nellie Melba? No, she
sings like every Australian — all the notes and
none of the music. Caruso again. Miss Alma
Gluck? That one's cracked. Geraldine Farrar?
Definitely not! Miss Mary Garden? Yes Yes, you
sing from the soul, Miss Garden. *(She puts the
record on the gramophone turntable.)* No, from
the *belly*, which is even better.

*(She cranks the gramophone and drops the needle
onto the lacquer surface of the record. MUSIC:
"L'amour est une vertu rare" from* Thaïs, *recorded
by Mary Garden in 1912. Sarah sways slightly
from side to side, "inhaling" the music.)*

SARAH: Yes! *(She hums along with the record for a
moment.)* Yes, Miss Garden, the sun! She's angry!
She's — very angry! And who could blame her?

(Pitou returns with a large blue folder, scraps and

*slips of paper protruding from it in every direc-
tion. He sees Sarah, frowns.)*

PITOU: *(Raising his voice above the music)* Our
notes, Madame.
SARAH: Shh! The music . . . the sun . . .!
PITOU: *(Louder)* Our notes, Madame!
SARAH: *(Fiercely, dismissing him) I see them!*

(She resumes her swaying. Pitou moves closer.)

PITOU: I thought we intended to work.
SARAH: I *am*, Pitou! I am remembering . . .
remembering my mother!
PITOU: One moment, Madame.

*(He sits quickly, begins pawing through the
notes.)*

SARAH: My mother! *(She laughs.)*
PITOU: Your mother . . .?
SARAH: My mother, Judith van Haard, was the
daughter of a Dutch Jew who made straw furniture. But she was ambitious. She became
French, Catholic, and a kept woman by the time
she was twenty.
PITOU: *(Still searching through the folder)* We
already have all that, Madame.
SARAH: *(Ignoring him)* She was a woman with
nothing to offer Life, except her beauty and her
good manners. I didn't inherit either. She was
devastated!
PITOU: *(He locates a large group of notes and
takes them from the folder. To himself)* Here she
is. "Mother."
SARAH: My mother was like . . .
PITOU: *(To himself, overlapping)* Filed under *P*
for "Parent".

SARAH: Like violets!
PITOU: Subfiled under *M* —
SARAH: Like a bunch of violets!
PITOU: For "Maternal."
SARAH: They have changed hands so often,
they've lost some of their freshness!
PITOU: "Maternal Parent" —
SARAH: But the chafing of all those hands has
heightened their perfume!
PITOU: I.e., "Mother."
SARAH: *(Aggravated at his mumbling)* Pitou! Are
you taking this down?!
PITOU: Of course, Madame.

(He scrambles for pencil and paper.)

SARAH: My mother was like violets from Holland,
wrapped in gauze and tissue paper. Their
fragrance is most powerful when they have been
crushed a little.
PITOU: *(Writing)* A little slower, Madame. From
"tissue paper."
SARAH: The record has stopped
PITOU: Thank God.
SARAH: Start it again.
PITOU: Madame —
SARAH: Start it again!
PITOU: You and Miss Garden at the same time?
I'll end up transcribing Massenet!
SARAH: *Start it again!*

*(Pitou sighs, crosses to the piano, winds the
gramophone.)*

SARAH: And where's my parasol?
PITOU: Your *what?*
SARAH: P—A—R—A—S—O—L!
PITOU: Parasol? It's inside.

SARAH: I wanted it *outside!*
PITOU: For what purpose?
SARAH: It's uncommonly hot! Aren't you hot,
Pitou?
PITOU: Extremely.
SARAH: *Well . . .?*
PITOU: Well . . .?

*(She stares at him; he stares back at her. Finally
she shakes her head in despair, rolling her eyes.)*

SARAH: Put Miss Garden on again!
PITOU: *(To himself)* Miss Garden, the Memoir,
the parasol! Madame is rambling this afternoon.
Exactly like someone with a *fever! (He starts
the record again.)* If she'd only allow me to take
her inside, we could proceed in a logical manner!
SARAH: Quiet!

*(MUSIC. Sarah presses one hand to her forehead,
squints, trying to recapture the memory. Pitou
returns to his chair.)*

PITOU: *(Consulting his notes, very loud)* From
"tissue paper"?
SARAH: My mother — was —
PITOU: "Tissue paper"?
SARAH: My mother — my mother was —!
PITOU: *(Desperately)* "Tissue paper"!
SARAH: Be quiet, Pitou! I am trying to remember!
I am — *trying* —!

*(The record continues. Sarah's head droops. She
clinches her fists.)*

PITOU: Madame . . .?
SARAH: It's no good! It's not going to work!
PITOU: *(Looking at his notes)* Something about

your mother and Holland and tissue paper. But
Madame must give me some indication how these
apparently unrelated topics fit into —
SARAH: *It's not going to work!*

*(She tears the record from the turntable and hurls
it across the terrace. Pitou ducks, a reflex action.
The record hits the stone balustrade and shatters
with a loud crackle. Pause.)*

PITOU: Poor Miss Garden. *(He bends down,
picking up fragments of the record.)* She sings
flat, but that's no reason to —
SARAH: Forget Miss Garden!
PITOU: And I suppose we'll need a new needle for
the —
SARAH: FORGET THE NEEDLE! *(Pause.)*
Pitou? We'll have to use our *other method*.
PITOU: *(Dropping the record fragments)* No,
Madame! Please!
SARAH: It always helps. You were hired to help
me!
PITOU: Why don't we call a halt for today?
Tomorrow we can make a fresh start.
SARAH: Don't your care about the Memoir?
PITOU: *(Proudly)* It was my idea! The second
volume of Madame's recollections. For the en-
lightenment of the civilized world, and America.
SARAH: Yes — we shall *improvise!* It always helps.
You — you, Pitou, shall be — my mother.
Nagging, scolding, whining — you do it so well.
PITOU: I'm not an actor, Madame.
SARAH: And I shall be able to remember *every-
thing!*
PITOU: Madame, I — I can't!
SARAH: *(Holding out her hands to him, a re-
hearsed gesture of supplication)* Pitou?
PITOU: *(Rapidly)* There is nothing in my contract

that requires me to impersonate Madame's
relatives and acquaintances! I informed Madame
of that fact the first time she suggested this nonsense and I feed obliged at the present time to
remind Madame of the terms of our —!

SARAH: *Pitou! You will do it!!*

(Pause.)

PITOU: How do we start?

SARAH: I am — twenty-seven years old.

PITOU: *(He starts to remonstrate, thinks better of
it.)* Just as you say, Madame.

SARAH: *(Improvising)* I am living in Paris, on the
Left Bank. With my lover Prince Henri de Ligne
and our darling little baby, our little Maurice. *(In
a different voice)* Where is Maurice?

PITOU: He took your granddaughters and Dr
Marot to fish for shrimp.

SARAH: Excellent, we won't be interrupted. Yes,
the sun — never mind! I am twenty-seven years
old. *(To him)* You are my beautiful mother —

PITOU: Madame, please —!

SARAH: *(Firmly)* You are my beautiful mother!
You've come to nag and whine and perform the
rest of your repertoire as you do regularly, every
month! You are one of the most glamorous
women in Paris, in France, which is to say, in the
world. You have achieved affluence, Maman,
and even — respectability? — by taking to bed
with you several of the most influential men in the
country. One at a time, usually.

PITOU: Madame!

SARAH: Currently you are the mistress of the
dashing Duc de Morny.

PITOU: I can't play someone's mistress!

SARAH: It's a game, Pitou! Pretence — the
Creator's chief gift! A game to jog the memory
under this merciless sun — without my parasol!

PITOU: The parasol, Madame? You need only ask!

(He starts out. She grabs him by the coat-tails, holds him fast. He turns.)

SARAH: Don't make this too difficult for me, Pitou.

(Pause.)

PITOU: No, Madame.
SARAH: You begin — *Maman*. Just as we did it before.
PITOU: But, Madame —
SARAH: Please! You are Judith Bernhardt. One of the most . . .
PITOU: *(Very quietly)* One of the most . . .
SARAH: Glamorous . . .
PITOU: *(More quietly)* Glamorous . . .
SARAH: Women in Paris.
PITOU: *(A whisper)* . . . women in Paris . . .
SARAH: That's it!

(Pause. Pitou turns his back on her for a moment, trying to "assume the character." Sarah watches him expectantly.

In each of his "roles" Pitou remains essentially Pitou, rather ludicrous at first, improving as he goes along. He lightens his voice a bit for Judith and gestures occasionally in what he considers an elegant demimondaine manner, but it is not his favourite, or best, role.

After a moment he turns around again, as Judith Bernhardt. He has picked up a small ornamental fan from the piano, uses it as a "character prop.")

PITOU: *(As Judith Bernhardt)* Mademoiselle

Sarah! You are twenty-eight years old!

SARAH: *(Her younger self)* Twenty-*seven*, Maman.

PITOU: *(Judith)* It's time you left the theatre to seek honest employment. You have responsibilities, obligations.

SARAH: *(Sotto voce)* Good, Pitou. *(In the scene)* My obligations are to myself, Maman!

PITOU: *(Judith)* Indeed? And what about —? What about . . .?

SARAH: *(Prompting)* What about my baby?

PITOU: *(Judith)* And what about your baby?

SARAH: *(Prompting)* And Prince Henri?

PITOU: *(Judith)* And this fly-by-night Belgian dandy! You don't imagine he'll give your brat a name?

SARAH: *(In the scene)* He loves me, Maman.

PITOU: *(Judith — getting into it more)* Oh, the nobility's always game for a quick backstage tumble, dear. He'll sing a different tune when his parents discover a smear of greasepaint on the family crest!

SARAH: *(Sotto voce)* Wonderful, Pitou! And now she'd start: "I've done my best to —"

PITOU: *(Himself)* I know — I know that bit! *(Judith)* I've done my best to keep us decent. Myself and both my daughters.

SARAH: *(In the scene)* You always cared more for Jeanne! She is your favourite, your pet!

PITOU: *(Judith)* And why not? Jeanne, my baby, my angel. Nervous, yes, but *infinitely* devoted!

SARAH: *(Laughing, out of the scene)* You can't tell me you're not enjoying this, Pitou!

PITOU: *(Himself)* Madame! How can I possibly continue this charade if you —?!

SARAH: I'm sorry! Go on!

(Pause. Again Pitou turns his back on her, "assumes the character.")

PITOU: *(Turning back around, as Judith)* Mademoiselle Sarah, you are the bed of thorns on which my heart rests uneasily! You would never listen, would never let me guide you.

SARAH: *(In the scene)* You wanted Jeanne and me to be perfect replicas of yourself, didn't you, Maman? A Dresden china bitch and her two china whelps!

PITOU: *(Judith)* Don't you dare speak to me like that! You've always been self-willed, impractical! You've always had absurd fantasies about yourself —!

SARAH: Maman —

PITOU: *(Judith)* About life! About *men!* Even when I found you eligible suitors, which was not easy, considering —

SARAH: *Suitors?* Is that what they were? I remember — I was fifteen when you presented me to that — that hirsute Monsieur Berentz! I'd never seen a man — I'd never seen an *animal* so unalterably corporeal! Bristly! He even had hair growing under his fingernails!

PITOU: *(Judith)* He had a fine business.

SARAH: Yes. He made rugs. From his own hair, I have no doubt!

(Pitou-Judith gives her a stricken look, turns away, launches into a "mother's soliloquy:")

PITOU: *(Judith)* Doctors usually advise mature women to avoid alcohol, sweets, and any prolonged exercise that might injure the spine. My doctors simply told me to avoid my elder daughter!

SARAH: *(Out of the scene)* That's it! That's Maman! Continue! *(Prompting)* "*Naturally* I was concerned —"

PITOU: *(Instantly taking the prompt, as Judith)*

Naturally I was concerned! I am a mother! I saw
Sarah evolving into a shrill, rebellious creature
with a harsh Semitic profile — which was not
really her fault — and a fetish for affectation
which her years in the theatre did nothing to
correct! Far from it. Then, having ruined her own
life, she proceeded to — to *vulgarize* my little
Jeanne, my baby, my angel, with —

*(During this speech, Sarah, her eyes rolling, clasps
one hand to her bosom.)*

SARAH: *Wait!*

(Pitou looks at her, uncertain where or who he is.)

SARAH: Take this down! Hurry!

(Pitou puts down the fan, races to his notes.)

SARAH: Maman — Maman would not let me
forget! She blamed me! For Jeanne! For
Jeanne's —!
PITOU: Yes? Ready!
SARAH: *(Rapidly)* My sister would say to me,
"Sarah, there's a carousel behind my eyes!" And
I'd know she was drunk again. Maman blamed
me. "Your sister never drank before you adopted
her into your theatrical tribe! Before you dragged
her off on your insane tours, to New York and
God-knows-where-else!" The truth is, I didn't
want Jeanne to come. She screamed at me,
threatened me. She said I was jealous, afraid she'd
show me up to the Americans. So I took her
along. Gave her a few small parts, odd jobs. Yes,
but we were talking about — about her *vulgariza-
tion*, as you called it, Maman. Her disease.
Perhaps it was my fault. I wonder if I *encouraged*

Jeanne's drinking — looked the other way because
— because I hated her? It's a fact! From the
beginning I *hated* her. Because she was given the
best clothes, the holidays, the facial massages with
fresh cream!

PITOU: A little slower, Madame!

SARAH: *(No slower)* Jeanne was given every
chance! I fought my way into the Conservatoire,
fought to stay there! While Maman and her
gentlemen laughed at me. But Jeanne —! By some
good angel she was given a face that was not a
joke. Jeanne was beautiful. Like Maman. You can
look like a Jew and be beautiful — or you can
look like a Jew and look like a Jew. Jeanne had a
nose that was just a nose. She had a mouth. She
had hair. I had only my eyes. Everything else I had
to *invent!*

PITOU: *(Writing, without looking up)* I can't
possibly keep up —!

SARAH: The public *expects* beauty! The public
expects — *everything!* Beauty and wit —

PITOU: Please, Madame, you're drifting away
from —

SARAH: And straight white teeth!

PITOU: From the topic! You were speaking of
your sister and her —

SARAH: All my life I have given to the public! I've
given them — I've given them . . . *(Pause.)* Given
them what, Maman? Given them what, Pitou?

PITOU: Which am I?

SARAH: *Pitou!*

*(He quickly riffles through the blue folder, pulls
out a sheet of paper. He reads from it, pomp-
ously.)*

PITOU: "For more than fifty years I have given the
people of the world the vibrations of my soul, the

pulse of my heart, the tears of my eyes. I have performed more than one hundred and twenty-five roles with uncompromising —"

SARAH: Stop! Stop, Pitou! What is that drivel? You make me sound like a national monument.

PITOU: I am quoting Madame herself.

SARAH: That cadenza — about *vibrations? I* said that?

PITOU: Last week. Word for word. I filed it under *P.* For "Prolonged Digressions."

SARAH: Well. I am less of a fool this week than last. That's progress. Now, Pitou, you're wandering again! Where was I?

PITOU: *(Looking at his watch)* Madame, it's nearly dinner hour —

SARAH: I'm not hungry.

PITOU: I am.

SARAH: I think, Pitou, you must assume the role of Maman once again.

PITOU: Now?

SARAH: Don't whine. You were exquisite in the part. Except for that smudge under your chin. That's definitely out of character.

(Pitou blushes, rubs his chin angrily.)

SARAH: Now I've hurt your feelings. Oh, Pitou, you're like one of those wiggly little things with big red eyes one finds under rocks. I'm really very fond of you.

PITOU: *(Not happy)* Thank you, Madame.

SARAH: Maman was saying to me . . .?

(She looks at him. He doesn't move. She snaps her fingers several times, loudly, near his ear.)

SARAH: Maman was saying . . .?!

(Pitou picks up the fan again, turns his back on her, then turns around again almost immediately.)

PITOU: *(Judith)* Mademoiselle Sarah, you are twenty-eight years old! It's time you —
SARAH: *(Inspired)* No! I am *eleven*.
PITOU: *(Himself) Eleven?*
SARAH: Play along, Pitou, play along!
PITOU: But you've never been eleven before! I'm not sure —
SARAH: Oh, my mother was the same at any age! I am eleven. *You* are twenty-seven.
PITOU: I became a mother at a very tender age.
SARAH: We are standing, my mother and I, before a gray wall that disappears into gray trees that disappear into a gray sky. Maman has brought me to the convent at Grand-Champs. She is turning me over to the nuns for domestication. She cannot endure my tantrums any longer nor my bad manners. I pinch her gentlemen friends in all the wrong places. I experience her rejection keenly. I am weeping.

(She puts one hand over her eyes and mimes sobbing, her body shaking.)

PITOU: *(After a moment)* What am *I* doing?
SARAH: *(Without looking around)* I can hear my mother speaking to Mère Sainte Sophie, the Superior of the convent.
PITOU: Speaking about *what?* We've never done this before. I don't know what to —
SARAH: *(Out of the scene, impatiently)* All right, all right, all right! Since you make everything so difficult! We'll try another way. You are no longer Maman!
PITOU: Thank God.

SARAH: You are Mère Sainte Sophie of the convent at Grand-Champs!

PITOU: No!

SARAH: Here. Put on this shawl.

PITOU: *No!*

SARAH: You *don't* care about the Memoir!

PITOU: That's not fair!

SARAH: Come along then! The shawl, yes.

PITOU: Couldn't I be a man?

SARAH: In the convent?

PITOU: The gardener? The postman?

SARAH: The shawl! *(She helps him arrange it over his head, like a wimple.)* There. Very saintly. Ethereal. Not of this world.

PITOU: What about your mother?

SARAH: Maman has gone. In her enormous black carriage. Listen! There it goes, rattling across the cobblestones in the courtyard. I am little Sarah Bernhardt. Eleven. Frightened to death. You are a tall gray woman with a voice like a clay jug thrown against a stone wall. You want to comfort me, calm me.

PITOU: How?

SARAH: Begin by getting my attention. I am in the corner of the vestibule, sobbing. Everything familiar to me has vanished in that black carriage! Speak to me. Reach out to me.

(Pitou grimaces, then turns his back, "assumes the new role." Sarah resumes her mime of weeping.)

PITOU: *(Turning back around, as Mère Sainte Sophie)* Mademoiselle Bernhardt . . .?

SARAH: *(Very young)* What do you want?

PITOU: *(He sighs, but continues as Mère Sainte Sophie)* Mademoiselle Bernhardt — you are eleven years old.

SARAH: *(Out of the scene, displeased)* Oh, Pitou!

PITOU: *(Himself)* It's the best I can do.

SARAH: But you start every scene the same way! "Mademoiselle Bernhardt, you are so-many years old."

PITOU: I didn't say "so many"!

SARAH: People don't talk like that!

PITOU: I'm not a dramatist!

SARAH: People don't begin every conversation by announcing the age of their listeners! You must have noticed that! What *would* Mère Sainte Sophie say, under the given circumstances, at the given time?

PITOU: I don't know any nuns!

SARAH: Try again.

PITOU: But, Madame —

SARAH: Don't whine! Concentrate! Here I am. Eleven years old. Weeping in the corner. Approach. Speak!

(Pitou approaches, starts to speak, produces an unintelligible noise. Pause. He tries again.)

PITOU: *(Mère Sainte Sophie)* Mademoiselle Sarah . . .?

SARAH: *(More or less out of the scene, watching him)* Yes . . .?

PITOU: *(Mère Sainte Sophie, struggling)* Mademoiselle Sarah — you are — you are weeping in the corner, I see?

SARAH: PITOU!

PITOU: *(Himself, throwing off the shawl)* That's it! That's all! I've had enough!

SARAH: *(With great force)* Very well. Let's throw away our notes! *Everything!* Press clippings, programmes, citations, invitations! This specimen collection of my life! Forget the Memoir! I can't do it without your help! I shall just lie here,

like an old lizard who hasn't much longer to
live!

PITOU: *(Overlapping, putting his hands over his
ears)* Stop — stop, stop!

SARAH: *(Rapidly, speaking between her teeth, a
habit)* I shall abandon my ambition — my dream
that I might — no, that *we* might, together, you
and I — salvage — even at this late hour! — some
meaning, some *truth* from my —!

*(Pitou has picked up the fan again. He hammers
with it on the piano, trying to drown out her
tirade.)*

PITOU: *(Overlapping the speech above)* Stop, stop!
Stop! Stop, stop, stop, stop, stop! *Stop* —!

*(He continues hammering and shouting for a
moment before realizing that Sarah is silent.
Pause. He looks at her, shamefaced, then at the
fan, which is in tatters.)*

SARAH: *(Accusingly, with tears in her voice)* That
fan, Pitou — was presented to me — at the Troca-
déro Gardens — during the Universal Exhibition
of 1878 — by the Emperor of Ceylon. It was made
of silk and monkey bones. It took thirty-two
Buddhist priests more than three years to complete
the design. Carving, staining, painting, polishing.
Fasting and praying. Then carving, staining,
painting, polishing some more. Then fasting and
praying . . . And so on.

(Pause.)

PITOU: I've had a terrible week. My kidneys.

SARAH: The priests in Ceylon are not responsible
for your kidneys. Nor am I.

(Pause.)

PITOU: All right. I'll be Mère Sainte Sophie and you —
SARAH: No! *(She stretches her arms, winces slightly.)* I'm tired.
PITOU: Shall I put on another record?
SARAH: *(She shakes her head "no".)* But I would love to have my parasol.
PITOU: At once, Madame.

(He starts out, stops as she speaks.)

SARAH: Yes. She *knows* she's dying.
PITOU: What?
SARAH: The August sun. She'll be extinct. In a mere billion or trillion years. I think she's punishing us, don't you? She's disappointed to discover she's not immortal.
PITOU: *(Nervously)* And — a cool drink, Madame?
SARAH: Yes. Please. Run along now. I'll just close my eyes until you get back.

(Pitou exits into the house. Pause. Sarah opens her eyes, stretches again, trying to relax. She takes the blue folder from the table, places it in her lap, thumbs through it.)

SARAH How on earth does he find anything in here? *Everything's* filed under *P.* "Productions." "Postcards." "Profanity." The scraps and treasures of a lifetime. He needs only one letter to classify them all!

(She takes an old theatrical programme from the folder, reads the note attached to it.)

SARAH: "Twenty-first of December, eighteen

seventy-four. Madame played Phaedra. First time
at the Comédie-Française. The critics were
ecstatic.''

*(She smiles, returns the programme to the folder,
places the folder on the table again.)*

SARAH: And *now?* Now I play children's games
with Pitou. Pitou — with a face that someone
drew on a blackboard. And fingernails that
haven't been trimmed since his confirmation.

(Pause. She looks out at the sun.)

SARAH: They *all* play games with me. Games to
amuse the ancient child. Now that her real life is
over. It's pathetic. Pathetic. *(Pause.)* And the
final game? The final performance? Her absolutely final appearance anywhere! Slipping
down into the earth. Not as I expected — all at
once, in a wooden box, shutting out the nuisance
of memory with a neat final thud! — but *gradually*
slipping down, a fraction of an inch every day,
every hour — coffined in a peeling skin which no
cream or kind words can remedy. Just *disappearing.* Without dignity. Slowly — disgustingly
— helplessly losing my grip on what is sharp and
solid. *(Pause.)* Is that . . . all?

*(She draws a quick breath between her teeth, bites
her lip — a pain, more severe than before. Her
eyes close. She slumps back in her chair. Pitou
returns with the parasol, rushes to her.)*

PITOU: Madame? *(Panicky)* Madame!

(She opens her eyes, smiles.)

SARAH: What?
PITOU: *(Relieved)* Your parasol.

(She takes it from him, lays it aside without looking at it.)

SARAH: And my cool drink?
PITOU: Cool drink?
SARAH: Never mind. You distracted me. I was remembering — that wonderful night at the Comédie. My first Phaedra.
PITOU: *(Quoting from memory)* "The critics were ecstatic."
SARAH: Oh yes. And they should have been!

(MUSIC: solo woodwind. Sarah looks out at the sun. Pitou sits at the table, looking through the folder for notes concerning Phaedra.*)*

PITOU: But I think we covered Madame's triumph as Phaedra in Volume One, didn't we?
SARAH: *(Suddenly, as Phaedra)*
        "I'll go no farther!—"
PITOU: *(Looking up)* Hmm?
SARAH: *(Phaedra)*
        "Stay and rest, Oenone!"
PITOU: *(Very quietly, to himself)* Mother Mary!
SARAH: *(Phaedra)*
        "I cannot move. My strength is all but gone.
        My eyes are wounded by the light of day!
        My faltering knees refuse to bear me up,
        Alas!"

(Pitou, watching her, shakes his head. As she continues, he begins browsing through the folder, paying no attention to her.)

SARAH: *(As Phaedra, her famous rapid delivery)*

    "These worldly jewels, these veils have
       weighed me down!
    What meddling hand has tied these useless
       knots
    That bind my braided hair across my brow?
    Yes, all of you conspire to grieve and wound
       me!"
(Looking out at the sun)
    "You, shining author of a tragic race!
    You, whom my mother —!"

(She looks at Pitou, who is absorbed in the folder.)

SARAH: *(As Phaedra, louder)*
    "O Sun! I come to gaze at you this one last
       time!"
(As herself) Pitou! *(He looks up.)* You're not
listening?
PITOU: I've heard Madame's Phaedra a thousand
times.
SARAH: *(Fiercely)* The scene is new every time I do
it!
PITOU: Madame knows my opinion of the classics.
Racine, Corneille! They didn't write about *real*
people. Not the people *I* know. Grown women
panting like draft horses, throwing themselves at
men's feet! Writhing. Perspiring!
SARAH: No one ever panted after you?
PITOU: I'm proud to say no one ever did.
SARAH: Well, that doesn't come as a complete
surprise. But you? Didn't you ever heave and
groan and — lose your buttons?
PITOU: Madame!
SARAH: You told me you were in love once.
PITOU: Yes. Once.
SARAH: I never heard any of the details. The
romance didn't mature?

PITOU: No.
SARAH: Tell me about it.
PITOU: It's a personal matter, Madame. I'm not
required by my contract to —
SARAH: *Tell me.*

(Pause.)

PITOU: *(Reluctantly)* I was twenty-five years old.
She was called Lisette.
SARAH: *Lisette.* Perfect.
PITOU: I had the greatest respect for her. And she
— loved me. She said she loved me.
SARAH: You were going to be married?
PITOU: In April.
SARAH: Perfect.
PITOU: I was twenty-five, and still —
SARAH: Still —?
PITOU: Innocent.
SARAH: At *twenty-five?*
PITOU: *I* was not in the theatre, Madame!
SARAH: *(She smiles.)* Of course.
PITOU: My parents adored her. Her parents
adored me. My old Aunt Isabelle had put down
a deposit for us, on an apartment in Belleville.
SARAH: The future was in your pocket!
PITOU: It was! *(Pause.)* I thought it was.
SARAH: But?
PITOU: It was — You could say it was "a
difference of opinion."
SARAH: Between you and Lisette? A difference of
opinion about what?
PITOU: About whether or not to — whether or not
we should — wait.
SARAH: Wait?
PITOU: Until after the marriage.
SARAH: Ah, you were too passionate, Pitou! Too
eager, too anxious?

PITOU: No. *She* was.

SARAH: *Lisette?*

PITOU: ''What harm can it do?'' she said. And she smiled. If you could have seen her smile! ''What harm can it do? In another month it will be legal and sacred. We're only cheating the Church of a few days, Georges.'' It seemed — logical.

SARAH: Yes. Absolutely!

PITOU: One very hot day — I didn't know her parents had gone for a picnic in the country — Lisette stayed behind, told them she had a touch of something contagious, wanted to stay at home and nurse it.

SARAH: Ah.

PITOU: She had arranged for me to visit her that afternoon.

SARAH: Ah.

PITOU: She met me at the door. Didn't say a word. She took me by the hand and led me into her bedroom. If you could have seen her bedroom!

SARAH: Lace, lots of lace?

PITOU: Acres of it.

SARAH: Perfect.

PITOU: She sat on the edge of the bed. She made me sit beside her. I tried to make small talk. I knew what she had in mind. I'm no fool, after all. But I still thought we should *wait*. Well, I had a conservative childhood. My mother used to tell me — *(Pause.)* This was years ago. Before all the formalities went to hell!

SARAH: Yes.

PITOU: Lisette said, ''Georges, you're being very foolish about this.'' And she —

(Pause.)

SARAH: And she —?

PITOU: I think I've said enough.

SARAH: Don't you dare stop now! You've just reached the climax! *(He gives her a stricken look.)* Sorry, the *crisis!* I must know the dénouement! *(Pause.) Pitou?!*

PITOU: We — Well, *she* took the initiative. She said, "Georges, let's both get comfortable."

SARAH: And you — got comfortable?

PITOU: . . . Yes.

SARAH: And?

PITOU: I was — excited at first! Who wouldn't be? I mean, *there we were —! (He gestures vaguely.)*

SARAH: Yes.

PITOU: And then — she began to — to laugh.

SARAH: Lisette?

PITOU: Yes.

SARAH: She had a lovely laugh?

PITOU: It didn't seem lovely that day!

SARAH: She was laughing — *at you?*

(He says nothing, looks away.)

SARAH: Oh, Pitou, what agony!

PITOU: And she just kept on laughing! My excitement changed to anger very quickly — then to embarassment. I — made myself *uncomfortable* again. And I left.

SARAH: Oh no.

PITOU: I only saw her once after that. When she told me she had decided to break off the engagement.

SARAH: No!

PITOU: "Georges," she said, "I had never seen a man before."

SARAH: Ah.

PITOU: "Georges," she said, "if *that's* what a man is, I just don't see how I could take marriage

seriously!'' *(Pause.)* And she began to laugh,
again! I said something unpleasant and ran away.
(Pause.) Someone told me she became an
illustrator of children's stories.

*(Sarah smiles, almost starts to laugh, but
suppresses it. She lays her hand on his.)*

SARAH: It's a touching story, Pitou. About *real*
people.
PITOU: *(Very low)* Yes.
SARAH: I really am touched. Oh, the world at
large thinks I have no human feelings, that I'm
only an old, crippled dragon, too ancient and
proud to — *(She looks out to sea. Suddenly, with
a child's fascination)* Pitou! The sun is going
down!
PITOU: Yes, it usually does, for the night.
SARAH: Going down into the sea! But at the same
time, the sun is coming up again. Somewhere.
PITOU: Couldn't we go inside now?
SARAH: In Japan or Manchuria.
PITOU: I'm *hungry*.
SARAH: The sun is a relative of mine. She must be.
Half the world is forever dozing. Except the sun
and me. We don't require sleep.
PITOU: May I get Madame her tablets?
SARAH: No. I won't close my eyes tonight until I
accomplish something. Every day now must
count!
PITOU: *(Wearily consulting his notes)* Phaedra?
SARAH: No. *America!*
PITOU: *Before supper?*
SARAH: *America!* The dust and the dollars! *(She
laughs.)*
PITOU: Madame, I feel obliged to comment on the
wayward nature of our work this afternoon.
SARAH: *(Overlapping, oblivious of him)* New

York! Virginia! Texas! California! Indians!

PITOU: Indians?

SARAH: Locomotives!

PITOU: *(He sighs.)* Locomotives . . .!

(He sits, resigned, takes up paper and pencil.)

SARAH: *(Very light voice, far away)* Somewhere
. . . in an American railway car . . . bridges and
tunnels and stars. The rest of my company has
gone to sleep hours ago. Even Sister Jeanne with
her bottle of gin cradled in her arms like a doll.
The terrible Mr Jarrett, my manager, has told us
in his terrible voice, "You people need your rest!
Go to bed, goddammit!" But I cannot rest. There
is someone in bed beside me. But I can't remember
his name.

PITOU: *(To himself)* I'm not going to write that
down.

SARAH: I am watching the lights from miniature
villages and miniature farms, racing across the
dark window. Miniature men on miniature horses
stop to watch Miss Sarah Bernhardt's private train
clatter past in the dust or snow. *(Her idea of an
American accent:)* "Oh yeah! Sarah Bernhardt!
Oldest woman in the world! Came over here and
got away with more loot than Billy the Kid!"

*(Pitou laughs quietly; so does she. It grows
darker.)*

SARAH: *America!* President Wilson. President
Roosevelt. President McKinley. They shot him,
and he had such a gentle face. *(Pause.)* And I met
Mr Edison. We got along beautifully. We dis-
cussed Shakespeare *and* electricity. *(Pause.)* And
Marguerite Gauthier, my "Lady of the Camellias."
God, how the Americans loved to watch that

woman die! Night after night. "Camille," they
called her. I don't know how they came up with
"Camille."

PITOU: *(Distastefully)* Americans.

SARAH: Mr Jarrett called it my "piggy bank role."
Whenever, wherever poor Marguerite's lungs
finally gave out, there was always a full house to
witness her demise!

*(She takes a large flower from a vase on the table,
puts it in her hair.*

*MUSIC: solo woodwind, continuing through the
next short scene.*

*Sarah suddenly falls back in her chair, closes her
eyes. Pitou starts to reach out and touch her,
concerned.)*

SARAH: "Listen, Armand! Dear one, you must
understand. I assure you, it is not so difficult to
die!"

*(Pitou takes a moment to realize what is
happening, then sits back, watching her. He likes
this play better.)*

SARAH: *(Marguerite)* "I am not suffering any
longer. How strange! I feel as if life were . . .
returning suddenly! Yes! I feel so much better
than I ever, ever have before! And — I shall live!
Oh, Armand, how well I feel!"

*(On the last lines she rises slowly, supporting her-
self on the table, smiling. Standing, she is very still
for a moment. Then her downstage fist clinches
twice, violently. Her downstage arm, in a spasm,
suddenly shoots into the air. After a moment it*

falls limp, and Marguerite's body relaxes in death.
Sarah falls back gracefully into her chair.)

PITOU: *(Softly speaking the last lines from the*
play) "Rest in peace, dear Marguerite. Much will
be forgiven you, for you have loved so much."

(MUSIC fades.)

SARAH: *(Her eyes still closed)* Curtain. *(She sits*
up, opens her eyes.) Pitou, you're wonderful! You
remembered Nichette's lines!
PITOU: I don't know if you recall, Madame, once
in Kansas City, when Madame's sister was —
indisposed — we thought I'd have to put on a wig
and play Nichette!
SARAH: *(Laughing)* Yes, I spent all morning
pouring foul black American coffee down the
stupid girl! To spare the public your debut!
PITOU: *(Offended)* I don't claim to be an actor!
It's you who insist that I take part in these — these
spectacles!
SARAH: *(Suddenly serious)* My God, the hours are
slipping away from us! Pitou? *(He looks up.)* I
have an idea!
PITOU: Oh no.
SARAH: You'll be Mr Jarrett now. Mr William
Edward Jarrett!
PITOU: But —
SARAH: It's evening. Late evening. Near —
Detroit. My train has stopped to allow a herd of
milk cows across the tracks.
PITOU: Milk cows?
SARAH: Mr Jarrett, that ferocious Englishman
who managed all my American tours till he died in
Panama — *of* Panama — Mr Jarrett knocks at
the door of my private car. I am resting.

(She reclines, then looks at Pitou, who frowns, doesn't move.)

SARAH: Mr Jarrett knocks at my door! Near Detroit. Late evening. *Suddenly I hear . . . ?*

(Pitou knocks, on the piano.)

SARAH: *(Younger voice)* Who's there, please?
PITOU: *(Himself)* Wait a minute.

(He turns his back, concentrates on the new role, then turns back around, using a pencil for Jarrett's perennial cigar.)

PITOU: *(Jarrett, gruff)* It's I, Miss Bernhardt! Mr Jarrett! William Edward Jarrett!
SARAH: I have retired for the evening. Good night, Mr Jarrett.
PITOU: There's something we must discuss, Miss Bernhardt!
SARAH: It can wait till morning!
PITOU: *(Jarrett)* Please let me come in, Miss Bernhardt!
SARAH: Absolutely not! I need my rest. Don't blame me if the schedule is arduous. Go away, Mr Jarrett!
PITOU: *(He shrugs. More as Pitou than Jarrett)* As you wish. Pleasant dreams.

(He sits.)

SARAH: Pitou!

(He stands.)

PITOU: Madame?
SARAH: It is vital that Mr Jarrett speak with me tonight!

PITOU: You sent him away.

SARAH: William Edward Jarrett would never slink away like a whipped cur! He would bluster his way into my car, yelling like a Cossack! "Bloody hell, Miss Bernhardt! Your so-called bloody delicacy can take the night off! I'm no bloody actor to be sent away with a wink and a promise!"

PITOU: I won't speak to Madame like that! I couldn't!

SARAH: It's not you, Pitou. It's Jarrett. "Bloody actresses, bloody Americans, bloody hotels!" That was his style, his unique charm.

PITOU: I will not say "Bloo-" — *that word!* I know enough English. It's not polite.

(Sarah rolls her eyes, angrily pushes the hair out of her face.)

PITOU: *(Rapidly)* Perhaps — perhaps I could substitute something less objectionable in place of *that word?* For example, instead of *that word* I could say, oh, some nonsense word, so that you and I would know when Mr Jarrett would have used *that word* but I'll be spared the anguish of speaking to a lady, such as yourself, in a manner unfit for a gentleman, such as myself, to speak to a lady —

(During all this, Sarah has been squirming. She growls, picks up a heavy cushion from her chair, and hurls it at Pitou with all her force. A direct hit. Pitou pauses, only momentarily, looks at her, stoops, picks up the cushion, smiles tentatively, and, keeping the cushion between himself and Sarah, continues even more rapidly.)

PITOU: For example, instead of 'I'm no *that word* actor," I could say "I'm no *so-and-so* actor!"

SARAH: *(Searching for something else to throw)*
Shut up, Pitou!
PITOU: Or — "I'm no *higgledy-piggledy* actor!"

*(She throws a large book at him. He wards it off
with the cushion.)*

PITOU: Yes! *(Jarrett's voice)* "Higgledy-piggledy,
Miss Bernhardt!" —

*(She throws a handbag which she snatches from
the table; Pitou dodges.)*

PITOU: *(Jarrett's voice)* "I'm no higgledy-piggledy
actor!"

*(She throws another, larger book. Pitou again
uses the cushion as a shield.)*

PITOU: There, that sounds better already, doesn't
it?

*(She raises a glass scent bottle, takes aim. Pitou
cringes behind the piano. Pause. She sets the
bottle down with a bang.)*

SARAH: Pitou . . . Forget Mr Jarrett's unique
charm. Forget "bloody". And *please* forget —
PITOU: Higgledy-piggledy?
SARAH: *Yes!* Simply say what Mr Jarrett would
say, leaving out *all* obscenities. Knock again, Mr
Jarrett, knock again!

(Pitou drops the cushion, knocks on the piano.)

SARAH: *(Immediately)* Come in, Mr Jarrett!

(Pitou "enters", swaggering, with his pencil-cigar.)

PITOU: *(Jarrett)* How did you know it was I, Miss
Bernhardt?

(She gives him a withering look.)

SARAH: I'm tired. What do you want?
PITOU: *(Jarrett)* What do I want . . .?

(Pause. He hasn't considered this.)

SARAH: Is it about money?
PITOU: *(More or less Jarrett)* About money . . .?

*(He looks at her, uncertain. She shakes her head
slightly.)*

PITOU: *(Jarrett)* No! No, not about money, Miss
Bernhardt!
SARAH: Is it about my animals? Someone told me
that my darling little Jasmine, my little friend
from the Congo, ate some of the upholstery in the
observation car. I can hardly be held responsible
for . . .

*(Her voice fades: she should have been inter-
rupted. Pitou looks at her. Again she shakes her
head.)*

PITOU: *(Jarrett)* No, not about the animals!
SARAH: What is it, then? Speak your piece, Mr
Jarrett, and evacuate my bedchamber! *What do
you want?*

(She stares at him.)

PITOU: *(Desperately, beginning to lose his grip on
Jarrett)* Surely *you* must know — what it's
about?!

SARAH: I have no idea!

(She stares at him. He is near the breaking point, when she finally speaks.)

SARAH: Unless you intend to trespass again on my private life? *(Pitou moves closer.)* Unless you've come her, driven by an Englishman's innate lack of tact, to speak about my sister? Or about — *(She bites her lip.)* — about *Jacques?*
PITOU: *(Recognizing his cue, relieved, as Jarrett)* That's it! About *Jacques!*
SARAH: *(Instantly in the scene, furious)* You have persecuted my husband from the start of this tour! Poor Jacques. I promised him he'd be happy in the theatre. You didn't even want to hire him as my leading man! Did you? Why not? You have something against Greeks?
PITOU: *(Jarrett)* Miss Bernhardt, this is your fourth American tour —
SARAH: Fifth!
PITOU: *(Jarrett)* You've never brought along the same *masculine luggage* twice! None of them was equipped with more, in the way of talent, than good legs and hair on his chest! Did I ever complain before? No! You never felt obliged to marry one of them before!
SARAH: But I'm in love with Jacques! Can't you understand —?
PITOU: *(Jarrett — getting into it)* Never mind "in love"! I'm talking about *money*, Miss Bernhardt! The only reason we come to this godforsaken country! Your husband is a *business risk*. I won't discuss his shortcomings as a human being. I haven't got the time. The fact is, at every performance, he can't remember his lines, can't remember his moves. Isn't it a fact that he has a weakness for . . . *chemicals?*

SARAH: Who's been telling tales?

PITOU: *(Jarrett)* The best thing for all concerned is to ship the poor fellow back to France, get him into a hospital where they can look after his sort!

SARAH: Jarrett, you're impertinent! You're using your very lucrative position as my manager to launch an attack on — on a fine man — a continental gentleman. And you won't even call me Madame Damala!

PITOU: *(Jarrett)* The public pays for Sarah Bernhardt! Not Madame Damala! And most certainly not for *Monsieur* Damala!

SARAH: *(Out of the scene, serious)* Yes, Pitou. You even have Jarrett's scowl. And you say the same *impossible* things he used to —

PITOU: *(Enjoying this role, not wanting to relinquish it, as Jarrett)* Now, now, Miss Bernhardt. Let's stick to one topic at a time! *(Carried away, he throws himself into it:)* One *bloody* topic at a time!

SARAH: Pitou!

PITOU: *(Jarrett)* Pitou can't help you now, Miss Bernhardt! I want some *bloody* answers and *bloody* fast!

SARAH: *(In the scene again)* I don't owe you any answers, Mr Jarrett! Nor my soul! Nor my courtesy if you persist in this —!

PITOU: *(Jarrett)* Not interested in your bloody courtesy! Not interested in your bloody soul either, except for that slice of it you barter across the bloody footlights for cold American cash!

SARAH: *Mr Jarrett!* You are forcing me to choose between you and my — and Monsieur Damala? I warn you, don't do this! You will lose. Jacques *is* my husband. You are only . . . Jacques is my . . . I don't care what you think — any of you! Jacques *is* . . .

(Pause. MUSIC: solo woodwind. Pitou watches her. It is nearly dark now. Sarah puts one hand on her side, closes her eyes. Her face is tight. She is in pain.)

SARAH: It was my sister Jeanne who introduced me to him. In Paris. Jacques Aristide Damala. But I fell in love with him afterwards. In Saint Petersburg. At the Casino.

(Pitou sits, begins taking notes, with difficulty in the semi-darkness.)

SARAH: He was winning then. He didn't need his — chemicals. He taught my son to cheat at cards, but Maurice still hated him. *(Pause.)* He had the most perfect beard I have ever seen! All Greeks are beautiful at thirty. *(Pause.)* Someone told me that he and Jeanne were — Before we met, that Jeanne and he — That it was Jeanne he really liked.

(Pause. She looks out into the last rays of the sun, takes a deep breath, relaxes a little.)

SARAH: When we are young, it is their bodies that attract us, that draw us to them. The flat stomachs. The large ankles, strong feet. The fur on their chests and shoulders . . . .
PITOU: *(To himself)* I don't want to hear this.
SARAH: Later we learn to appreciate the masculine mind . . . such as it is. The masculine atmosphere — cigar smoke, honour — alcohol and insolence. *(Pause.)* In our last years — where I have arrived — not without mistakes — it is their *bodies* again. Eh, Maman?
PITOU: *(Very softly)* Maman again?
SARAH: In our last years — where I have arrived —

without even wanting to — we are gargoyles,
carved in old flesh — reaching out for something
— someone young!

(Pause.)

SARAH: Jacques! *(Pause.)* Jacques? *(Pause.)*
Jacques . . .!

*(MUSIC: a single high woodwind note that
continues for a long time. Pitou puts down the
notes, crosses to her.)*

PITOU: Madame. *(He touches her arm.)* Madame?
SARAH: *(Taking his hand)* Don't call me that,
Jacques. You make me feel old. Bad form for a
lover. Worse for a husband. Someone told me that
Greeks are the best lovers. Except for Swedes, and
who can take a Swede seriously? What are you
thinking, Jacques?

(Pitou starts to move away. She won't let him go.)

SARAH: *(She laughs.)* I've frightened you. Don't
leave me. Come closer. Look at me, Jacques. Is
that so difficult?

(Pitou looks at her, very anxious.)

SARAH: How old do you think I am? Go on, guess.
I'll give you one hint: I never met Louis the
Fourteenth. *(She laughs.)* Now, guess. Guess my
age, Jacques!
PITOU: *(Quietly, serious)* Seventy-five?
SARAH: *(She laughs.)* Jacques, *seriously!*
PITOU: Thirty?
SARAH: I'm thirty-eight.
PITOU: Really?

SARAH: I've taken good care of my skin. That's
the one thing of any importance my mother taught
me. And a woman of my sort mustn't burn herself
to a cinder in a few years. A woman like me wants
to *last*. Kindness helps. You'll have to be kind.
PITOU: Everyone is kind to Madame.
SARAH: Put your arm around me, Jacques. Now.

*(Pitou starts to do so, reluctantly. Noise offstage,
within the house — voices, laughter, clatter. A few
lights will shortly appear on the main floor of the
manor house.)*

SARAH: What's that?
PITOU: Monsieur Maurice and the others!
SARAH: Never mind Maurice. He's just a boy.
He'll learn to love you, Jacques. Give him time.
PITOU: Shall we go see if they caught any?
SARAH: Caught any?
PITOU: Shrimp.
SARAH: *(She laughs.)* What are you talking about?
I never know. *Put your arm around me. (Pause.)*
Tell me the things you told me our first night
together.
PITOU: *(Still quieter, frightened)* Madame —
SARAH: Jacques?
PITOU: *(Pulling away from her)* We can work on
the Memoir tomorrow.
SARAH: *Jacques . . .!*
PITOU: *(A whisper)* No, Madame. It's *Pitou*.

*(She turns and looks at him. She leans very close
and stares at him in the twilight. Pause. She makes
a small sound of disappointment and turns away.
MUSIC: solo woodwind.)*

PITOU: They'll be asking for you. Your granddaughters. They've planned fireworks — fireworks

and God knows what else, out beyond the garden.
I think we should go inside now and . . . I think we
should go inside.

SARAH: Yes — *you. You* go inside. Go on.

PITOU: And you'll — be all right for a while?

SARAH: I have always been all right. When I'm
alone.

*(Pause. Pitou starts out, stopping as he passes the
table to pick up the blue folder and the parasol.)*

SARAH: My parasol. You're not taking that?

PITOU: Yes.

SARAH: Idiot! The sun! I'll turn speckled as a
Brittany hen!

PITOU: *(Quietly)* The sun's gone down, Madame.
It's dark.

(Pause. Sarah looks all around.)

SARAH: Leave my parasol. It's a merciless moon
tonight!

*(Pause. He brings her the parasol, which she
opens and holds above her head. Her face is in
shadow.)*

SARAH: Pitou — you're not still here?

PITOU: No, Madame.

(He exits quickly into the house. Long pause.)

SARAH: *(Eventually)* I threw . . . all the pillows . . .
off our bed. I didn't even want *them* between us.
His eyes were closed. "Are you asleep, Jacques?"
"No." "What are you thinking?" "Nothing."
"We'll be happy, won't we, Jacques? We won't
spoil all this . . . will we?" *(Pause.)* He laid his
arm across my breast.

*(Pause. Sarah bites her lip, clinches and un-
clinches her fists several times. She moans softly.
After a considerable struggle, she relaxes again.
Pause.)*

SARAH: *(Softly)* I came to love the convent. In
time. Mère Sainte Sophie and the gray sisters,
perfectly still at night on their hard gray beds,
waiting for Jesus and death. I came to love that
life — that lack of life. And I begged Maman to let
me stay, to let me die there with the sisters. *(A
younger voice)* "Oh, it won't take long, Maman. I
will die very young, I know that. My young soul
will rise in the pure air, toward the perfect light of
the stars!" *(Pause. She looks up into the darkness,
very angry.)* I didn't know then that you were
burning yourselves to cinders! I thought that *you*
at least were *immortal!*

(Pitou returns, crosses quickly to her.)

PITOU: They're asking for you, Madame.

(Pause.)

SARAH: I know.

(Pause.)

PITOU: Monsieur Maurice says I'm to bring you
in, whether you want to or not. *(Pause.)* They're
all asking for you.

*(Pause. He takes her arm. They move slowly
toward the house. She clutches the parasol, holds
it above her head. In the distance, beyond the
manor house, fireworks begin to glow regularly
across the night sky.*

MUSIC: solo woodwind. Then a particularly brilliant burst of colour and light somewhat nearer. Sarah lowers the parasol.)

SARAH: Dear God! What was that, Pitou? Not the sun again! Already?

END OF ACT ONE

ACT TWO

The terrace. Night. Darkness, except for two or three small smoky hurricane lamps. Half an hour before dawn.

Sarah, in a long nightgown and robe, is at the piano, playing the same three bass notes over and over and over.

The blue folder is on the table. Several handfuls of notes have been removed from it, and a few loose papers are scattered across the flagstones.

SARAH: *(As she plays)* Charming. *Charming.* *(She continues the three notes. Now she adds an odd, crooning melody with her right hand.)* I composed it for my son. For Maurice. A lullaby. How simple it is. The left hand never changes. Just those three notes. Just those three.

(The sea is heard. She stops playing.)

SARAH: The wind's churning up a storm out there! I can smell it. I love a good storm!

(She plays a few more bars of the lullaby, then stops abruptly, slams her fists down on the keys.)

SARAH: No! Maurice always despised my lullaby. Even when he was an infant, it made him scream! *(Pause.)* I'll surprise them all! I'll — *accomplish* something! Every — day — now.

(She crosses to the table, sits, draws the blue folder closer to her, rummages through it.)

SARAH: I'll make sense of all this — somehow. No one else can be expected to.

(She takes a group of notes from the folder, holds them close to the lamp, squints.)

SARAH: *(She reads:)* "Eighteen eighty-three." My God! The Ice Age! Was I alive then? *(She squints at the notes again, reads:)* "Twelfth of December, eighteen eighty-three. Publication in Paris of — 'The Wicked Life of Sarah *Barnum*' — by Mademoiselle *Marie Colombier!*" *(Angrily she throws the notes down.)* Treacherous, black-hearted bitch! After I took you into my confidence — tried to make an actress of you, taught you everything! I should have used a shotgun on you, Colombier! Oh, the filth you wrote about me in your scabrous little book! *(She recites from memory, venomously:)* "Regardless of her fame, the divine Sarah is merely a homely, ill-mannered nymphomaniac Jewess. A false metallic goddess whose brazen talents were forged in the furnace of Deceit for no higher purpose than Quick Profit — a common obsession of her tribe!" *(She snatches up the notes again, squeezes them in one fist.)* I should have spilled your blood, *Colombier!*

(Pause. She straightens the notes a bit, holds them near the lamp again.)

SARAH: *(She reads:)* "*Thirteenth* of December, eighteen eighty-three. Madame inflicts retribution." *(She laughs.)* I adore the word, Pitou. *Retribution!* Yes! I grabbed my horsewhip, given to me by Canrobert, the Grand Marshal of France! I took Colombier by surprise, at her home! Oh, God, I only inflicted one or two solid blows before the filly fled! *Vanished!* Afterwards I was told that she secreted her ample figure in her potato bin. But — I *demolished* her apartment!

I must have resembled an avenging angel! *Retribution!* I tore down her dirty mauve window curtains — imitation velvet! I ripped up the cushions of her hideous horsehair sofa! I tore them with my teeth! Yes, *with my teeth! (Pause. She catches her breath.)* I had very good teeth then. I still have.

(Pause.)

SARAH: Naturally, the newspapers made the most of that episode. And every other episode — real or imaginary — public or private! "Mademoiselle Bernhardt, is it true that your affection for your pet tiger verges on what might be called the unnatural?" "Is it true you sleep in a coffin, usually in the nude, and not always alone?" "Madame, we have been informed by a reliable source that your husband, Jacques Damala, was arrested in Nice this morning and charged with assault, indecent exposure, and trafficking in narcotics! Would you care to comment?" *(Pause.)* And of course — when my leg was taken off — oh, that was a field day for the *gentlemen of the press!* One of them — he must have been English — called me "Long John Bernhardt"! *(Pause.)* All this mirth. At the expense of a very old ... and crippled ... woman.

(She takes a deep breath, bites her lip.

MUSIC: the same woodwind phrase as in ACT ONE, but played in reverse, falling from high to low.

The sea is heard, more faintly than before. Sarah looks up at the sky.)

SARAH: Not a single star up there. Burnt out

already? No. But they've deserted this whining little earth — taking our angry sun with them. They didn't give *us* a second thought. *(Pause.)* Why should they?

(She picks up a single sheet of paper from the pile on the table, reads:)

SARAH: "Eighteen ninety-one. Madame is received by Her Majesty Queen Victoria." *(She smiles, remembering.)* And she *never* saw theatre people. She manoeuvred me into a corner, swore me to secrecy, and confessed she was learning to play poker — had a passion for it! *(Pause.)* But she's dead now. *She's* dead too.

(She drops the sheet of paper, sifts through the loose notes, picks up a very small scrap.)

SARAH: *(She reads:)* "Nineteen hundred and eleven. Florida. A Red Indian chief. Madame takes a canoe ride." *(Immediately she wads up the scrap and throws it away.)* I didn't like that smelly old crocodile of a man! He told the interpreter I reminded him of his grandfather! *In war paint!*

(Pause. She digs into the folder again, takes out several pages pinned together, reads the top page:)

SARAH: "Eighteen ninety-nine. The end of Monsieur Damala. Collapse — and death."

(She closes her eyes, takes a deep breath, opens her eyes, looks at the page again.)

SARAH: Yes, Jacques. It was *you*. *You* taught me this — sordid fear — which I must find a way to

live with tonight. *You* made me "face the facts!"
Those were your words, Jacques. Lying there on
that filthy cot, in that airless room on the rue
d'Antin. The floor was littered with ampoules of
morphine and cocaine! Your *body* — which had
been an object of worship for me, Jacques! —
your body was pockmarked with needle scars.
Some of them had already become swollen, in-
fected. You looked at me from under your bruised
eyelids — and you smiled. Idiot! You said, "You
must face the facts. Always *face the facts*,
Madame Damala! I am killing myself — yes! —
and I don't give a damn for your theatrical grief *or*
your pity! I need money to finish this. Will you
give me some money, Sarah? For old times' sake?
Otherwise, *get out of my sight!*"

*(Pause. She looks at the notes. She is weeping.
Pitou enters from the house, in trousers, dressing
gown, and slippers. He sees Sarah, stops, rubs his
face with both hands. He remains in the background, watching her intently.)*

SARAH: "The end of Monsieur Damala." *At last!*
I felt only — relief! — when they told me you were
gone at last, Jacques. Seeing Death across from
me at the breakfast table — and in the corner of
my room just before I blew out the last candle at
night! — I couldn't live like that! God help me! I
still have not come to terms with — *all that!* I
can't! I — can't —!

*(She sobs and buries her head in her arms on the
table. Pitou adjusts his robe, crosses quickly to
her. He pauses beside her. She does not see him.
He turns his back on her for a moment, then turns
back around, using a pencil as his cigar:)*

PITOU: *(Jarrett)* Bloody hell, Miss Bernhardt! I
must speak to you about — about your relations
with these — these goddamn gigolos!

SARAH: *(Raising her head)* What are you doing —?

PITOU: *(Himself, desperately)* Play along,
Madame, play along! *(Jarrett)* Miss Bernhardt,
there's no question you're the most appealing,
most fascinating bloody female on earth!

SARAH: No!

PITOU: *(Jarrett)* But these worthless young men,
no matter how bloody pretty they are —

SARAH: It's no good!

PITOU: *(Jarrett)* You have a duty to your public!

SARAH: *(Overlapping) Pitou!*

PITOU: *(Jarrett, overlapping)* For more than fifty
years, you've given them the vibrations of your
soul —!

SARAH: *(Overlapping)* Listen to me!

PITOU: *(Jarrett, overlapping)* — the tears of your
eyes! You are beloved by every bloody creature on
this bloody planet!

SARAH: *Listen, Pitou! (Pause.)* I am grateful for
what you're trying to do. But I'm not a child to be
humoured by these old flatteries, yours *or* Mr
Jarrett's. *(She looks at the disarray of notes on the
table.)* I want to make sense of all this! I want to
understand! *(Pause.)* I'm going to die very soon.

PITOU: *Impossible.*

SARAH: Oh, you *men!* You eat and sleep and make
love and drop dead without the least sense of
occasion! But a woman of my sort has an instinct
for timing. *(Pause. She takes a handkerchief from
her sleeve and wipes her face.)* I am going to die
very soon.

PITOU: You promised your granddaughters you'd
live to be at least a hundred and three!

SARAH: *(She smiles weakly.)* I never kept

promises. *(She looks at the soiled handkerchief.)*
Pitou . . .?
PITOU: *(Quickly)* Yes? Madame will go to bed
now?
SARAH: *No.* My makeup box. My paints. Fetch
them.
PITOU: *(Looking at his watch)* Does Madame
realize it's nearly five o'clock?
SARAH: My powder and pencils!
PITOU: At least let's get you inside!
SARAH: My paints, Pitou! I mustn't be seen like
this.
PITOU: Seen? By whom?
SARAH: *My makeup box! Now.*

(He starts toward the house.)

PITOU: *(Just loud enough for her to hear)* I shall
wake Monsieur Maurice.
SARAH: You leave Maurice alone! Idiot!
(Suddenly, in a different voice) Did they catch any
shrimp? Maurice and the girls?
PITOU: Only a few. Your son presented them to
you at supper, but you wouldn't eat.
SARAH: They didn't go to the right cove. They
were afraid. *(Proudly) I'm* the only one who
knows how to climb down those rocks! *(Pause.
She looks at him.)* Why do you stand there with
that look on your face — like a lump of tallow
when the wick's burnt out? I asked you to fetch
— something!
PITOU: *(Intentionally vague)* Oh?
SARAH: You know perfectly well I asked for my —
What was it I asked for? *(He shrugs.)* YOU
WERE HIRED TO HELP ME! Go and fetch it at
once, whatever it was! I'll — I'll remember what
it was when I see it! Understand?

PITOU: I haven't *understood* more than ten
minutes of the past week!

*(He exits into the house. Pause. Sarah glances
down at the notes.)*

SARAH: "The end of Monsieur Damala." *No!
(She pushes the Damala notes far away from her
on the table.)* No more. No more, Jacques! On a
night like this — with the stars gone forever! — I
should be remembering — one of my triumphs!
One of "the great Bernhardt's endless triumphs."

(She searches through the blue folder.)

SARAH: Yes! "Performances." "Extraordinary
Performances?" What's he put in here?

*(She takes out a theatrical programme on which a
memo has been scrawled.)*

SARAH: *(She reads:)* "Eighteen ninety-nine.
London. Madame accepts a great challenge . . ."
(She reads a bit more, then laughs.) They said I
wouldn't dare. Not in England! That I wouldn't
have the "unmitigated audacity"! I was
determined to make it a *triumph!*

*(MUSIC: solo woodwind. Sarah strikes a
"masculine pose.")*

SARAH: *(As Hamlet)*
"Oh that this too, too solid flesh would melt,
Thaw and resolve itself into a dew!
Or that the Everlasting had not fix'd
His canon 'gainst self-slaughter! O God! God!
How weary, stale, flat, and unprofitable
Seem to me all the uses of this world!

Fie on't, ah fie! 'tis an unweeded garden
That grows to seed; things rank and gross in
   nature
Possess it merely . . . ."

(Pause. She relaxes out of the pose.)

SARAH: *(Herself)* It's too easy — too easy to say
those words tonight. They don't seem like lines
from a play at all. *(She smiles bitterly, baring her
teeth.)* Max Beerbohm called me "Hamlet,
Princess of Denmark." The dog! But he was
kinder than Mr Shaw. They were *all* kinder than
Mr Shaw! My God, I want to outlive that man!
George Bernard Shaw is one person whose funeral
I would forgo all other entertainments to attend!

*(Pause. She looks out at the sea, which is heard,
very faintly.)*

SARAH: Ah, but the French — *my* French — they
still love me. They will *always* love me — both my
legs, or only one! *(Pause. Her face tightens in
anger.)* PABLO!

(Pitou returns with a large makeup case.)

SARAH: It was all your fault, Pablo!
PITOU: It's I, Madame. *Pitou.*
SARAH: *(Gesturing toward the notes)* Take this
down, take this down exactly!
PITOU: *(Offering the case to her)* Madame's
makeup?
SARAH: I don't want that!
PITOU: But Madame insisted —
SARAH: Put it down, put it down, put it down!
PITOU: *(Doing so)* It's down, it's down, it's down!
SARAH: I am — *remembering* —

PITOU: Mother Mary!

(He rushes to the table, finds a pencil and paper.)

SARAH: *(Rapidly)* Rio de Janeiro. Nineteen hundred and five. October . . . ninth! I was playing La Tosca by Sardou. And the audience was with me that night, through all of Tosca's rapture and torment! The Muse was there! The President of Brazil was there. Where were *you*, Pablo?

PITOU: *(Looking up from the notes)* Pablo?

SARAH: *(Quietly, excited)* The final scene! Tosca must not be taken prisoner to be tortured and violated by the secret police. *Trapped!* She throws herself from the highest turret of the Castel Sant' Angelo into the swelling Tiber below! I'd done it a thousand, thousand times. But that night — where was *Pablo?!*

PITOU: *Pablo?*

SARAH: That damned stagehand! I should have killed him!

PITOU: *(Nods and continues writing.)* Ah — *Pablo.*

SARAH: It was Pablo's only duty to place my big mattress beneath the canvas battlements of Sant'Angelo! Leaping to her "death," Senhora Bernhardt was to fall only eight feet, and into a Tiber stuffed with goose down. But that night — the mattress was not in place. Senhora Bernhardt fell eight feet — onto one knee — on the hard-wood floor. *(Pause.)* Oh, I took my curtain calls as usual that evening. And Pablo and I laughed together about the missing mattress. Though my right knee was already beginning to swell a little. For ten years after that, I had doctors to diagnose, massage, burn, freeze, plaster, and give up hope on my knee. Then, during the Great War, I was

playing Jeanne d'Arc in the provinces. I heard the
cue for my first entrance — but —! "Dear God!
Maurice! Someone! I — I can't walk! *I can't walk
at all!*" They carried me to my dressing room and
sent for one of those *eternal* doctors! Oh, I had
every sort of doctor, at one time or another.
Everything but a veterinarian. Maybe I should
have tried one of those. *(She smiles ruefully.)*
This particular doctor was young — and shy —
and somewhat cross-eyed.

*(Pause. Suddenly she leans across the table, puts
her hand on Pitou's arm, speaks to him softly:)*

SARAH: Well? What's to be done now, Doctor?

(Pitou looks at her, startled.)

SARAH: What's to be done?
PITOU: Madame —
SARAH: I want the truth, Doctor! I am a rational
creature, whatever you may have read to the
contrary. My leg will have to come off? Is that it?

*(Pitou rallies a bit, starts to protest, but before he
can:)*

SARAH: *Is that it?*

(Pause.)

PITOU: *(Wearily, speaking for the Doctor, no new
voice)* . . . Yes.
SARAH: When?
PITOU: Well . . .
SARAH: The sooner the better?
PITOU: Yes.
SARAH: You're afraid of infection? *(She looks at*

him. Pitou nods.) Then you'll have to take —
almost *all* my leg? Above the knee? *(Pause.)* Oh,
God, Doctor! What a — what a *thing*. Mère
Sainte Sophie used to say I had a colourful phrase
for everything, including a number of things no
young Catholic lady should mention. But I admit,
at this moment, to a sudden loss of vocabulary.
What a *thing! (Pause.)* How is it done, Doctor?
Describe the process to me.

PITOU: Describe —?

SARAH: *Amputation.*

*(She searches quickly through the folder, takes out
a long, brown envelope, offers it to Pitou. He
doesn't take it.)*

PITOU: Madame, it isn't — A doctor is not
required to tell his patient —

SARAH: I am a student of life, Doctor! Every real
artist is! I've witnessed hundreds of operations.
During the war with Prussia, I set up an emer-
gency hospital in what was left of the old Odéon
Theatre. Men were horribly burnt and torn. *(She
thrusts the envelope toward him again.)* Well,
Doctor . . .?

*(Pitou looks at the envelope, shakes his head
violently.)*

PITOU: I just — I just can't!

SARAH: Can't?

PITOU: *Can't!*

SARAH: Doctor, I want to *face the facts!* I *need*
the facts, to replace the shame and shambles of
memory! And I will not rest until you give me the
facts I require!

PITOU: You will not . . .?

SARAH: Rest.

PITOU: Until —?
SARAH: *No.*

(Pause. Pitou sighs painfully, takes the envelope from her, removes the document inside, looks at it, clears his throat.)

PITOU: *(He reads:)* "Report of Military Surgeon Major Denucè, attached to the hospital at Bordeaux. February, nineteen fifteen."
SARAH: I am acquainted with your name and the date, Doctor. Proceed with the details of the operation. *Every word.*
PITOU: *(He reads:)* "Due to the potential hazard of gangrene — in Madame Bernhardt's case — I used an open or 'guillotine' amputation." Madame!
SARAH: Now, now. You're a doctor.

(She sees the makeup case, pulls it nearer, opens it, takes out several small jars of paint.)

SARAH: *(To him)* Continue.
PITOU: *(He reads:)* "I made a circular incision — seven and three-quarter inches above the knee."
SARAH: Continue.

(She begins to apply a harsh white paint to her cheeks and forehead.)

PITOU: *(Forcing himself)* "I severed the skin and subcutaneous tissue — and allowed them to retract. I divided the deep fascia and muscle in thin layers."

(Pause.)

SARAH: *Continue.*

PITOU: "I cut — the bone —" *(He stops, swallows hard.)* "Nerves and major blood vessels were lig— lig—"
SARAH: "Ligated."

(She daubs her lips with carmine.)

PITOU: *(Slower and slower)* "I — removed the limb — leaving a stu— *stump* — which — Leaving a stump which —"

(He looks at her. She is applying the finishing touches to her makeup. He slams the document down angrily, moves away from the table.)

PITOU: *Why am I doing this?!*
SARAH: Because you were *hired* to *help* me!
PITOU: *Help* you?

(She has finished making up, the caricature of a young girl. In limelight she might appear more youthful. In the strange light of the oil lamp, she is a grotesque. She takes a mirror from the lid of the case, looks at herself, then turns to him.)

SARAH: Look at me, Pitou. Come closer!

(He crosses to her reluctantly.)

SARAH: Tell me. Am I —?
PITOU: *(Quickly)* Yes! You're radiant as ever!
SARAH: Liar!
PITOU: *(Desperately)* What do you expect me to say?

(She looks into the mirror again, smiles suddenly.)

SARAH: Pitou! You know whom I look *exactly* like?

PITOU: Your granddaughter?

SARAH: That drab little insect?

PITOU: Madame!

SARAH: *Wait? (She grabs a stick of black makeup from the case.)* Time now for a *new* game — which we shall call — "Guess Who, Pitou."

(She hastily draws a thick black line above and below each of her eyes. She puts her face very close to his, grins hideously.)

SARAH: *Guess who, Pitou!*

PITOU: Saint Theresa.

SARAH: You're not trying! No, I'm that marvellous mime from the Left Bank! You know! He was all the rage in the sixties!

PITOU: *I* wasn't born in the sixties!

SARAH: That clown with the marvellous ugly avian profile, they used to compare it to mine! *You know!*

PITOU: At this hour I can't even recall my own name!

SARAH: *(Overlapping, suddenly flinging out her arms in birdlike manner) Le Corbeau!* Caw, caw, caw! Le Corbeau! Remember?

PITOU: Never heard of him!

SARAH: Caw, caw, caw! *Le Corbeau!* And he did that wonderful routine in which — No, wait! I'll do it for you!

PITOU: *(Rubbing his eyes)* I know I won't recover from this!

SARAH: Le Corbeau's most celebrated routine! *(In a barker's voice)* Ladies and gentlemen! A chance to see yourselves as others see you! Le Corbeau will now demonstrate something we *all* love to do! What? *(She slaps playfully at Pitou, as if he were a wag in the audience.)* No, no, monsieur! It's not *that!* Shame on you! We can't show *that* onstage! *(She laughs breathlessly, then raises her voice*

again:) Le Corbeau will show us what we spend
most of our time doing, all of us, every day!
Watch! See if you recognize what it is!
PITOU: Mother Mary!
SARAH: Ladies and gentlemen! *Le Corbeau!*

*(She applauds and signals for Pitou to do the
same. He applauds perfunctorily, unhappily.*

*MUSIC: a French vaudeville tune, far in the dis-
tance. Sarah "makes an entrance," as Le
Corbeau. Pitou watches. She ambles forward a
few steps in a lopsided corvine fashion, then seats
herself slowly, carefully, on the edge of a chair.
She becomes very very still. Pause. And that's it
— the whole routine. She merely sits, completely
motionless, for a long time. Pitou stares at her,
dumbfounded. After at least twenty seconds of
total immobility, she glances at him, falls out of
the pose. MUSIC fades.)*

SARAH: Don't you see? They gave him a superb
introduction, got the audience so excited! And
then — he just sat there! *(She breaks up.)* And we
laughed — my Jesus!

*(She laughs very hard for a moment, then stops,
looks at Pitou, who looks back at her blankly.)*

SARAH: *(As though to a child)* The announcer
said, "It's what we spend most of our time doing,
all of us!" See?! It's *nothing!*
PITOU: I understand, Madame. I just don't
happen to find it funny.
SARAH: *(Spiteful)* What *do* you find funny?
PITOU: At five o'clock in the morning?!
SARAH: If you won't laugh at what *I* think is
funny, then you must have your own *theory*,

Pitou, about what is funny and what is not! Let's
hear your *theory!*

PITOU: One's sense of humour is personal! I'm not
required by my contract to —

SARAH: *(Fiercely)* I have served the public for
fifty-five years! I have made them weep, faint,
gasp — and *laugh!* But perhaps *you*, Pitou, can
teach *me* what people react to, what is really
funny!

PITOU: Madame —

SARAH: Your *theory*, Pitou! *I'm listening!*

(Pause. Pitou thinks it over.)

PITOU: *(Flatly) Nothing* is not funny. *Something*
is.

(Pause.)

SARAH: That's it?

*(He nods. She clinches her teeth, snatches a small
towel from the makeup case, rubs at the black
lines above and below her eyes, smearing them.)*

SARAH: *(Between her teeth)* Well, what can I
expect from Life but *idiocy?* That has become its
basic ingredient!

*(She throws the towel down, picks up the mirror,
stares into it.)*

SARAH. My God — this isn't a face! It's gray mud.
It *was* a sort of face, before the years began to
rain down on it. Now it's only a *muddy rag!* With
five holes in it!

(Using the mirror, she suddenly bats the makeup

case off the table. It crashes onto the flagstones.
Brushes and little pots of paint scatter across the
terrace.)

SARAH: It's *worse* than death, Pitou! Inventing
these games to pass the night! Holding on — with
my teeth and with my nails! — to the games! —
now that my real life is over! I'd rather *die now*
than wait it out!

(Savagely she shoves several handfuls of notes off
the table.)

PITOU: I knew this would happen!
SARAH: No one listens!
PITOU: I *knew* in five minutes you'd be —
SARAH: That's right, *don't* listen! Shut me out! I
want you to shut me out! I did not *ask* to pass
through this late hour, like an old dream that
troubles the sleep of the children! And you are
all my *children* — who cry out to me in the night,
"MOTHER!" Not because you need me! But
because I *terrify* you! *(Suddenly very quiet)* Some-
thing shapeless — in gray flesh —! I am *dying*,
Pitou. And I am afraid!
PITOU: Madame Bernhardt! I'm going for the
doctor!
SARAH: No!
PITOU: Or Monsieur Maurice!
SARAH: *No!*
PITOU: This madness, it's every night now! It used
to be once or twice a month, but *now* —

(She grabs him with one firm hand.)

SARAH: Feel how *strong* it is, Pitou! The bone and
muscle inside the gray mud! How can *that* die?!
PITOU: Madame!

SARAH: *And I am not mad!*
PITOU: *Please!*
SARAH: I am not mad *yet! Understand me?!*
PITOU: *No!*

(He pulls free. She slumps back.)

PITOU: I'm going — I'm going to fetch your
medicine at least!

*(He runs into the house. Pause. Sarah looks down
at the makeup case, the scattered paints, papers,
and so on, all around her. She starts to move
away.*

*All at once she shudders — her entire body
shaking. She gasps, stabs one hand into her side,
the other into her bosom. She bites her lip, hard.
Pause.)*

SARAH: *Pitou . . .! (Pause.)* Pitou —?

*(She moves forward a little farther. She gasps
again, louder. She sways, closes her eyes. Pause.
She opens her eyes very wide. A look of anguish
crosses her face. She screams hoarsely. She falls.
She exhales a long, dry breath. She appears to be
dead. Pause. The sea is heard.*

*Pitou returns with a large bottle of pills in one
hand, a glass of water in the other. He sees Sarah,
panics, rushes to her.)*

PITOU: Madame!

*(He sets the bottle of pills and the glass down on
the table, kneels beside her, takes her face in his
hands.)*

PITOU: *Madame?*

(Pause. He takes his hands away. Her head falls back, lifeless.)

PITOU: Madame Bernhardt — if you're —!

(He feels frantically for her pulse. Nothing. He stands, in tears.)

PITOU: *In God's name —!*

(He starts to back away, slowly at first, his eyes on her constantly. Then he turns and starts toward the house at a run. At the same time Sarah stirs slightly.)

SARAH: *(Without opening her eyes)* Pitou . . .?

(Pitou stops, turns, not certain whether he's actually heard anything. Sarah does not move. He crosses a step or two toward her.)

PITOU: Madame . . .?

(Pause.)

SARAH: Pitou? Are you — there?

(He rushes to her, crouches beside her. Unable to speak, he helps her to stand, holds on to her. He is weeping.)

SARAH: Pitou —?
PITOU: Madame! I'm — I'm sorry. I thought you were — I thought —
SARAH: I think I know — what you thought. Shh!
(She reaches out slowly, touches his face, then

puts her hand on his neck.) Oh, poor Pitou. *(She laughs softly.)* You look worse than — than poor Jacques when I discovered him in that hotel room. He'd been unconscious for three days.

PITOU: Let me help you.

(He slowly guides her to a chair, helps her to sit. It is a long and awkward process. There is no sound for several seconds except their laboured breathing and the soft incoherent sounds of their struggle. Finally Sarah is seated again. He props her up with cushions, gently helps her to straighten her clothing.)

SARAH: Was I — gone — a long time just then, Pitou?

PITOU: I don't know how long it was. I only know I was certain that you —! What would I have said? How could I have explained that it happened while I should have been with Madame? That I was even, to an extent, responsible for it?!

SARAH: *(She smiles.)* No one is responsible for me. Not at my age. *(Pause.)* I'm a little cold now.

(Pitou quickly fetches a large bulky brown fur from the bench, tucks it around her. She takes his hand, holds it tightly.)

SARAH: It was — a wonderful thing, Pitou. Full of wonder! I could still hear you. I could feel you touch my face. But your voice and your hands were very far, *very far* away. I have never been so afraid. But it was, in a way, *wonderful. (Pause. She runs her fingers through the long fur.)* I shot this dreadful beast myself, you know.

PITOU: I know.

SARAH: In Oregon, I think it was. A rain forest where the moss hung down like an old Greek's beard. This monster came toward me, fangs dripping, huge hairy arms outstretched. I squeezed the trigger and shot him square in the chest! He looked astonished, that I would try to stop *him*, a force of Nature. Then he staggered forward another ten steps. I fired again, hit him in the chest again, almost in the same wound. And a new look came into his eyes. I could see that he was afraid but — full of wonder! In the last instant of life, he *grinned* at me. He leaned to one side, then the other. And he fell! *(Pause.)* Yes. He *grinned*, Pitou.

(Pitou looks around at the night's debris strewn across the terrace. Her eyes follow his.)

SARAH: I've made a mess.
PITOU: Yes.
SARAH: I'm sorry.
PITOU: I should go inside now, fetch Dr Marot to take a look at you.
SARAH: *No. (She gestures toward the liquor cabinet.)* I'll have a brandy instead.
PITOU: At this hour?
SARAH: I'm not counting hours anymore. A brandy. Not too small. If I sip it, it should last all morning.
PITOU: Wouldn't a glass of cordial be better? Or sherry?
SARAH: *Brandy*, Pitou.
PITOU: There's nothing harder on the heart than brandy. On an empty stomach?

(She looks at him steadily. He crosses to the liquor cabinet, pours a medium-sized brandy.)

PITOU: My mother wouldn't allow brandy in the house. She used to tell my father, "If you want to kill yourself, why not drink *arsenic?*"

(He brings her the brandy. She takes a long sip, smiles.)

SARAH: Your mother was a fool, Pitou.

(The light on the terrace continues its very gradual increase.)

SARAH: And now — there is something I *must say*.
PITOU: I'm listening, Madame.
SARAH: No, there is only one other creature on this earth who could understand completely what I must say now. I want to speak with him.
PITOU: With him?

(She takes another sip of brandy, looks at Pitou.)

SARAH: *Oscar Wilde*.
PITOU: Oh no — please —
SARAH: Yesterday you complained I don't let you portray enough men!
PITOU: But — I'd rather be a woman than Oscar Wilde!
SARAH: You're lucky he doesn't hear you say that.
PITOU: Oscar Wilde is dead, Madame.
SARAH: *Dead?* Oscar Wilde? Maybe you're right. So you're not only speaking ill of an author, but of the dead. Both mortal sins!
PITOU: Not as mortal as some that were indulged in — perhaps *invented* by Mr Wilde.
SARAH: I never believed all those stories.
PITOU: It was in the newspapers.
SARAH: You know how *I* feel about newspapers!
PITOU: But, Madame — *Oscar Wilde!* I don't deny what he wrote was sometimes very funny, but —
SARAH: Well, if he made *you* laugh, or even smile, that's no minor achievement.
PITOU: But —
SARAH: I am *remembering*. *(He is silent. Pause.)*

The Riviera — eighteen ninety — ninety-some-
thing — the last time I ever saw Oscar Wilde. He
was sitting on the beach, memorizing the
Mediterranean. A perfect time and place to speak
quietly about the things that matter. Sit, Pitou.

*(He doesn't move. She looks at him, very tired,
pleading.)*

SARAH: *Please.*

*(Pitou sits where she has indicated, on the
balustrade, downstage.)*

SARAH: I came up behind Oscar. I was the last
person on this earth he expected to see! Oscar is
watching three young bathers dash through the
spray.
PITOU: I'm sure at least two of them are boys.
SARAH: What difference does that make?
PITOU: None to me. To Mr Wilde, considerable.
SARAH: No. Oscar is old and sick now. All his
transgressions and triumphs are behind him. He's
come to Saint-Tropez for the sun. And to escape
his creditors.

*(MUSIC: solo woodwind, as in ACT ONE, rising,
rising. Sarah touches him gently on the shoulder.)*

SARAH: Hello, Oscar.

*(He looks up at her, then turns away for a
moment, to "assume the role." He gives Wilde a
voice that is quiet, androgynous, exhausted, with
a touch of British. It is probably his best
characterization.)*

PITOU: *(Turning to her, as Oscar Wilde)* My dear

Sarah. *Divine* Sarah. You are the last person on this earth I expected to see!

SARAH: I enjoy taking people by surprise, Oscar.

PITOU: *(Wilde)* We've both done that. All our lives.

SARAH: Yes.

PITOU: *(Wilde)* And now I think we must not die. Ever. That would be the greatest surprise of all.

SARAH: I'll — think it over.

(The both laugh, quietly.)

PITOU: *(Wilde)* Unless you can arrange to be struck by lightning, Sarah, during one of your immortal moments onstage. That is the only fitting way for you to depart this life. If you choose to depart at all.

SARAH: What about you, Oscar?

PITOU: *(Wilde)* No question about it. I hope to expire during an orgy.

SARAH: *(Sotto voce)* Pitou!

PITOU: *(Himself)* I'm doing my best.

SARAH: Well — never mind. "During an orgy." Perhaps he would have said that. How *did* Oscar die? Do you know?

PITOU: *(Himself)* Horribly. Swollen like a toad, unable to keep down a mouthful of food for five days before the end.

SARAH: I don't want to hear that! *(Pause.)* Poor Oscar. *(In the scene again)* My God, Oscar, you're red as a plum! How long have you been sitting out here?

PITOU: *(Wilde)* I don't remember, my dear. A long time. My rooms are so empty nowadays, I can't bear it. The conversation in the bar is tedious. Especially the conversation about me — always in a loud whisper.

SARAH: Was it dreadful for you — in prison?

PITOU: *(Wilde)* Yes. And disgustingly good for me. The plain life. The plain food. The plain guards.

(She smiles.)

SARAH: I wept for you, Oscar.
PITOU: *(Wilde)* Did you? Sarah Bernhardt wept for me? Perhaps it was all worth it, then.
SARAH: *(Pleased)* Oh, Oscar.
PITOU: *(Himself)* I think Mr Wilde meant it as a joke, Madame.
SARAH: It doesn't matter how he meant it, only how I understood it! *(Pause.)* Listen, Oscar. There is something I *must say* to you. Now.
PITOU: *(Wilde)* I'm listening, my dear.
SARAH: . . . The nineteenth century, Oscar!
PITOU: *(Wilde)* What about it?
SARAH: Torchlight. Candlelight. Lamplight. Privacy. Caviar, out of the fish and onto the table! Clothes that did more than just cover one's nakedness. Funerals to which it was not necessary to send invitations. We are the last of our kind, Oscar Wilde! The last Romantics. The last bright banners of ego and happy selfishness. Victor Hugo is dead. And Napoleon — all the Napoleons. Byron. Garibaldi. Robert E. Lee. They are all dead. People are very different now. So busy. So worried. So *democratic*. Searching for decisions that will pacify everyone and please no one. We weren't like that, Oscar. We lived exactly as we chose, every moment of our lives. We died young, at whatever age. The world may not have been a better place because we were in it. But it was larger — more interesting — more *innocent*. The people today — they know too many things. They have discovered that the sun is engaged in the long process of burning herself to a cinder. And they

can never forget that fact now! Do you think they
will understand what it was like, for us, to live
without that knowledge? To be so *alive* that *Death*
was the only thing impossible to imagine? *(Pause.)*
Death. *(Pause.)* Will they read about us, Oscar?
Will they remember?
PITOU: *(Wilde)* Possibly.
SARAH: Well, never mind. They'll have plenty to
worry about, without our Memoirs.
PITOU: *(Wilde)* All the same, I wrote one.
SARAH: So did I. I've started on my second
volume, in fact. With my secretary. A deplorable
little billy goat of a man named Georges Pitou.

*(Pitou looks around, wounded. She smiles.
MUSIC: solo woodwind.)*

SARAH: Good-bye, Oscar. Don't sit in the sun too
long. It's bad for the skin.
PITOU: *(As Wilde, but sounding very much like
himself)* Oh, someone will surely come to drag me
inside, when it's time to eat — or *sleep*.

*(Sarah waves, moves away from him. Then she
starts suddenly, as if stung by something.)*

SARAH: *Pitou!*
PITOU: What?
SARAH: The sun is rising!
PITOU: Yes.
SARAH: I can smell the sea! All the way up here.
PITOU: Dead fish.
SARAH: But the storm has missed us completely.
What a shame.

*(Pitou stands, blows out the lamp on the table,
begins retrieving the makeup, collecting the
scattered notes, and so on.)*

SARAH: They didn't catch any shrimp, you said?

PITOU: Not many.

SARAH: Cover your mouth when you yawn.
There's only one place to go for a good catch this
time of year. This afternoon we'll all tramp down
to the Apothecary's Grotto — what a delicious
name. Pitou — I believe I'm getting my second
wind!

PITOU: *(Horrified)* Madame will spend today in
bed. *Please*. I'll speak to Dr Marot —

SARAH: Don't you dare! He'd be fluttering around
all day with his smelly prescriptions. And he
makes the most obscene proposals. Just to make
me laugh, don't you think?

PITOU: I think he's been in love with you for years.

SARAH: Oh, everyone has, Pitou. Everyone. *(She
laughs.)* What a self-satisfied old bitch she is!

PITOU: Madame?

SARAH: The sun!

PITOU: Oh.

SARAH: Take this down, Pitou. For the Memoir.

*(Pitou, flustered, sits quickly, pushes some
crumpled notes aside, pencil and paper ready.)*

SARAH: *(Gazing at the sun)* I want the world to
know that I issued a challenge to that old gypsy to
come down from the heavens, to have it out with
me on the subject of immortality.

(Pitou looks up, puzzled.)

SARAH: But she is too *smug*. She continues to rise
and to set, thinking she is the only one with any
answers! *(Pause. Still looking at the sun, she
smiles, defiantly.)* I also have my answers. *(She
turns to him.)* Aren't you taking this down?

PITOU: That — that rigmarole — about the

sun? Do you want people saying you're senile?

SARAH: *(After a moment's thought)* Yes. I think that would be nice. Saves me the bother of being polite. *(Pause.)* Pitou? In the bottom right-hand drawer of my escritoire you'll find the manuscript of a new play. A young poet sent it to me last winter. I didn't think I'd have time to do it. I've changed my mind.

(He looks at the notes in his hands.)

SARAH: We'll continue the Memoir this evening, when we return from the grotto. It's August, Pitou. Long warm days. Plenty of time. *(She stretches her arms, looks at Pitou, who hasn't moved.)* Bring me that manuscript now. Then you'll take a letter to my young poet. He'll have to alter the age of his leading character a bit if I'm to play the part.

PITOU: Madame, a little breakfast first? Don't you think? Possibly a nap?

SARAH: Bottom right-hand drawer!

PITOU: Yes. *(He starts to go, then turns back.)* But I have to say — it seems to me — to make his leading character older may violate your poet's intention.

(Pause.)

SARAH: I want him to make the character *younger*, Pitou.

(Pause. He stares at her.)

SARAH: I want to *grin* at Death.

(Pause. He smiles, a very small smile, as bewildered by her as ever.)

SARAH: *Bottom right-hand drawer.*
PITOU: At once.

(He exits quickly into the house. Pause. Sarah turns to face the light.)

SARAH: Yes. *The sun.* Warm and constant as ever. As if the night and a slow death were fantasies told to a child.

(She throws her head back, looking directly into the source of the morning heat.)

SARAH: *You.* Yes, *you! You* aren't afraid yet? *Tell me!* Just a little bit *afraid?*

(Pause. She laughs, as though in acknowledgment of a positive response.)

SARAH: Yes?

CURTAIN

BODIES

by
James Saunders

BODIES

Bodies, commissioned by the Richmond Fringe Theatre, was first presented at the Orange Tree Theatre, Richmond, on 29 April 1977, directed by Sam Walters with the following cast:

DAVID	*Geoffrey Beevers*
MERVYN	*Rio Fanning*
HELEN	*Isobil Nisbet*
ANNE	*Ruth Goring*

On 20 February 1978, after ten previews, Hampstead Theatre staged it with the following cast:

DAVID	*David Burke*
MERVYN	*Dinsdale Landon*
HELEN	*Anne Stallybrass*
ANNE	*Gwen Watford*

Directed by Robin Lefevre
Designed by Tanya McCallin
Costumes by Lindy Hemming
Lighting by Alan O'Toole

Ray Cooney, by arrangement with Hampstead Theatre, presented *Bodies* at the Ambassadors Theatre, London, on 23 April 1979, after previews from 11 April, with *Angela Down* playing the part of HELEN, and lighting by Alan O'Toole and Gerry Jenkinson.

CHARACTERS

ANNE

MERVYN

HELEN

DAVID

The action takes place in the living-rooms of Anne
and Mervyn, and Helen and David.

ACT ONE

The living-rooms of Anne and Mervyn, and of Helen and David

(Anne enters)

ANNE: I was never, thank God, an Idealist; no romantic; the dewy-eyed approach irritated me. I suppose the parents contributed, with their talk of love and niceness, their comfy-cosiness, covering a shoddy making-do with each other. My first period, I thought: so that's what's behind it all — *this* discomfort, *this* mess. And these things sprouting in front, these impositions, to be hiked about, hawked about through life in case I should happen to breed. The nerve! Pretty brash cynicism; but better that way than the other. Useful too, a good defence, it gave me an edge, I used it when the time came, when the occasion warranted. "I'm having a period, do you mind!" They minded, mostly; well, at that age. Another trick I had, toffees in the handbag; faced with an importunate male at the end of a dreary evening he thought I should pay for, I'd pop a Sharp's Kreemy into my mouth and start chewing. That spiked the romantic gun, at the expense of a filling or two. Or both together, the ultimate deterrent. *(She talks as if chewing toffee)* "I'm having a period, do you mind!" I grew out of it, of course, matured; I mean I learned to enjoy myself, take what was available, including *romance*, why not; feet on the ground, though, head below the clouds, I thought I was unfoolable, set for life. My expectations were never more than reasonable, before and after marriage; I anticipated difficulties, and got them; I coped. His first infidelity — though I didn't believe in the concept — I pushed out of sight, refusing to be disturbed. And the others. And then, well into what I thought was my maturity, coming up forty would you believe, the cataclysm. The mess. The mess of it. I was not unhappy, that was the point, not dissatisfied as far as I knew, there were no great blisses but what do you expect, *I* expected nothing more; and then, out of nowhere, the first intimations: a restlessness, a strange unease, like the feeling you have before you know you're going to be sick. I increased my activity, became rather manic, threw a big party; I hated to be alone, doing nothing; time was going by so quickly, suddenly, *had* gone by, forty years of it, probably more than I had left. My time was running out, I had to use it, mark it with my brand. Something in me started looking for a meaning, a value that would give meaning, to make it all right that I was getting older and would die, die and lose everything. Be lost. Then it focused, oh so suddenly, or I became aware of it suddenly, focused on someone I'd known for years, one of our closest friends, David of David and Helen, our old buddies who lived in our pockets and we in theirs. It was ridiculous; ludicrous . . .

Helen enters

HELEN: I'd felt for some time there was something odd, something out of key, a vague disquiet; I thought it was me. Because on the face of it things were going better than usual with us. We were doing more together, going out a lot, entertaining, seeing a lot of Mervyn and Anne. We'd always gone very well together, the four of us. David and Mervyn were old buddies, and the first time I ever met Anne I knew we'd be good friends. I looked

up to her, she was older than me. I looked up to
her. We saw each other constantly about that
time, the two of us or the four of us: coffee,
shopping, P.T.A., cinema, drinks, meals, parties,
a lot of parties around then. One evening Anne
rang. She wanted to see a film, Mervyn wanted to
stay in, would I like to come. I said I couldn't, I
had something to do; I suggested David. "Oh,
yes," she said, "if he'd *like* to." I put him on the
phone, thinking perhaps I'd said the wrong thing:
she sounded rather uncertain. Then David: "Yes,
all right. Yes, that will be quite nice." Casual,
rather offhand. He put the phone down. He had a
large Scotch before he went. Halfway through the
evening the penny suddenly dropped. I realized I'd
known for some time. He came back saying how
dull the film had been; they'd had a coffee
afterwards. It had been going on for months.

David enters

DAVID: It seemed rather a small thing at the time.
Don't misunderstand; there was an intensity there,
a great physical attraction; but it didn't seem —
important, not vital, just something I felt would
be nice to happen, something I fancied. Things
were going smoothly enough marriage-wise; The
job was — all right, not unpleasant, not un-
interesting on the whole, I was doing quite well,
on my way up; and domestic-wise — well, as I say.
Kids set problems, of course, of course they do,
it's part of the game; but no great hassles, no great
dramas; we coped reasonably well together, we all
did. And I had my extra interest, if things got too
much, the creative outlet, the painting. There were
occasional frustrations there, I suppose: trying to
go beyond my talent, the odd loss of confidence,
but that's part of the process. Again, I don't want

to exaggerate, I didn't suffer with it. I was no Van Gogh, thank God, and knew it. A Sunday painter, I suppose; nothing wrong with that; if someone called it a hobby I didn't object. What I'm getting at is this: if at the time, when the thought first came into my head, when I first became aware of the attraction, the possibility — if then I'd thought through the possible consequences, the complications, I'd have said forget it then, sod it, I can do without it, I'll stay as I am, thank you very much.

Mervyn enters

MERVYN: I don't know when it started, I'd always assumed she was an attractive woman — most women are — but I'd never *noticed* she was. I began to remember details about her, the way a painter would, the shape of the fingernails, the colour of the eyes, the way she held her head, and the details had a kind of value, as they would to a painter. I'm not observant, I've always dreaded witnessing a crime, seeing the robbers leave the bank, being asked by the police: what exactly happened, what time was it, what did the man look like, was he wearing a hat, was he clean-shaven, is this him? So it was unusual, how she came into focus; I could have painted her from memory — if I could paint. Then I found I enjoyed talking to her, just me with just her, without the usual worry: am I boring you, do you really want to be talking to me? She listened, listened very intently, watching my mouth, letting me talk, hanging on my lips you might say, it was very pleasing. I found I was flirting with her; she was an old friend, the others were always there, it was an unspoken joke between us, no harm in it . . . One night we were coming back from the theatre, the four of us, in my car. Anne was in the back with David, Helen in front with me. I could hear them talking behind me, about the play, about theatre. Helen was quiet. I had a feeling I'd had before, of something passing between us; something was being said. She lit me a cigarette, put it in my mouth, her fingers touched my lip for a moment. The silence went on, while the others chattered in the back. I flashed a look at her face; she was watching my hand on the wheel, very intently. That's when I realized that she — desired me, and I her, and that we both knew; that the way was open. The tension was extraordinary. I changed gear, and left my hand there as if casually, the back of the hand brushing her skirt.

David is reading

HELEN: Guess who rang today.
DAVID: Hm?
HELEN: Guess who rang up today — Mervyn.
DAVID: Mervyn and Anne, Mervyn?
HELEN: Yes.
DAVID: Well, well — what on earth made him do that after all this time?
HELEN: He said he'd heard we were back in England, and thought he'd give us a ring.
DAVID: I'm surprised.
HELEN: I was.
DAVID: How are they both? Well?
HELEN: I think so.
DAVID: Still living in the same place?
HELEN: Mm.
DAVID: Old Mervyn . . . It would be nice to see them again.
HELEN: Do you think so?
DAVID: Why don't we?
HELEN: It's a long time.

DAVID: What is it — eight years?

HELEN: Nine.

DAVID: Do you think they'd like to see us? We could ask them over.

HELEN: Actually they've asked us. For a meal on Saturday. I said a provisional yes.

DAVID: Fine. We're not doing anything Saturday, are we?

HELEN: No.

DAVID: Funny, I was thinking about them only the other day.

HELEN: Were you?

DAVID: Something reminded me. It'll be interesting, seeing them again.

HELEN: Talking over old times?

DAVID: Hardly, I should think. Are you not sure about it?

HELEN: I just wondered what you'd think about it.

DAVID: It suits me.

HELEN: What are you reading?

DAVID: Detective.

HELEN: Good?

DAVID: Hm.

HELEN: Do you want to go out tonight?

DAVID: Where to?

HELEN: Cinema?

DAVID: I'm quite content to stay in. Are you going?

Slight pause

HELEN: I might.

DAVID: Is he still at the same school?

HELEN: We didn't talk much. He had to ring off, some crisis. I think he said he's a headmaster now.

DAVID: I think I'll ring him up.

HELEN: No, don't do that.

DAVID: Why not?

HELEN: I said I'd ring back. He said no, I'll call you tomorrow. He was ringing from school. So I'm to say yes.

DAVID: Yes, why not?

HELEN: There are all sorts of possible reasons why not.

DAVID: Not now, surely. I'm quite looking forward to it; seeing old Mervyn again.

HELEN: And old Anne again.

DAVID: Yes.

HELEN: Whoever *they* are.

DAVID: I don't suppose they'll have changed much. Nine years isn't all that long.

HELEN: That's just it. They won't have, we will have. They'll be the first of the old friends we'll have met since coming back. Rather going in at the deep end.

DAVID: It's always interesting, renewing old ties.

Helen gives a little cough

You know what I mean. No danger of *that*.

HELEN: *(fey)* You know you may do as you like, darling. *(She smiles)* It's odd, isn't it, that now we may both do as we like, we no longer want to?

DAVID: We do do as we like.

HELEN: *You* know what *I* mean. *(She kisses his forehead lightly)*

ANNE: It was bad. It got worse. I felt as if I were being taken over. Part of me of course wanted to be, wanted to give over control. And the arguments with myself: I'd be taking nothing from Mervyn; on the contrary, I'd be replenishing myself, it would be good for our relationship, make me a better wife. Perhaps I'd learn a new trick or two. Forgetting he'd said rather similar things to me, from time to time. At least I'd keep it to myself, at least I wouldn't come crawling home to confess, shove it on his shoulders, as he used to: "Darling, I have something to tell you . . .." Or moon about with that hangdog look of guilt on him, forcing me to prise it out of him, not having the courage, or the decency, to take his own responsibility, to take the trouble even to lie properly. Always imagining, it seemed — I never understood the stupidity of this — always imagining the time would come when I'd say, "You poor darling, how difficult it must be for you, I see how you need it, you must have it of course, you must be yourself, I quite understand." At least, I told myself I'd never do that; if David went with deception, that was the price to pay. And if he did find out, if there was even the danger, I'd stop. I was quite definite on that. And anyway — I said — I know there's a revenge in it, a getting my own back for various things; but better out than in. Better this little revenge that does him no harm than a soured bitter life later on. I'd be doing him a favour; and myself. Too many reasons. We all had too many reasons. I shuffled the cards, laying them out like a fortune-teller, trying to find the arrangement which would say: don't blame yourself; stop struggling; there's nothing you can do; it's ordained. Well, ordained or not, I went ahead and did it.

DAVID: That wasn't straight. To say it didn't seem important, to say it was just something I fancied, to say if I'd seen the difficulties I'd have done without — that was how I thought *then*, how I kidded myself. The part I played then, the act I put on, was of the carelessly trendy rising young executive; but — this was the clever part — not obsessed by it, not taken over, always my own man. I wasn't *in* the rat race, I just used the machinery to earn a living. Agreed, I'd say, arguing with Mervyn, the business ethic is a

questionable thing, or at least a frivolous thing; of
course I know marketing paper products is a
strange use of energy, if someone needs paper they
don't need me to tell them; but so's cricket a
strange use of energy. It's only a game — for me; I
don't take it seriously, as you do teaching; and
you don't believe in the education system. So with
the painting: I'd never allow I was serious at it. I
was everyone's man, and no-one's. I was, of
course, terrified: of not being noticed, not being
praised, not being liked, loved, admired, of being
caught backing a losing cause. Of not existing;
and no-one ever guessed, least of all me. I was
certainly no Van Gogh; but I suffered, suffered
the pain of not being told at every moment that I
was *necessary*. To business, to art, to Mervyn, to
Helen — and then to Anne. As soon as I saw that
to her I was an object of desire, I was done for; I
had to be the best, the greatest, the only, the
necessary lover.
MERVYN: Crisis today.
ANNE: Oh? What happened?
MERVYN: We had the police round.
ANNE: Not again. Shoplifting?
MERVYN: No, worse. You remember Simpson?
ANNE: Your weird sixth-former? Drugs?
MERVYN: No. He tried to kill himself.
ANNE: Oh my God.
MERVYN: Well, it seems that way. There were two
witnesses. He drove his motor-bike straight into a
wall. Revved up, and went straight into it.
ANNE: It could have been an accident. Perhaps he
skidded.
MERVYN: He didn't skid. He had perfect control.
They both said it looked totally deliberate. It was
a straight road. He's had the bloody bike two
years, he knows how to use it. And he'd left his
helmet off.

ANNE: How is he?

MERVYN: He's in a coma. They've got him on one of those life-support systems. He's not expected to come off it. *(He breaks a little)*

ANNE: Were you fond of him?

MERVYN: I hated the sod . . . No I didn't; I was sorry for him.

ANNE: Do you know why he did it?

MERVYN: The reason I'm a bit . . . The reason the police called round — with his father — was that it happened yesterday straight after school. During school in fact. He had a blank last period. Instead of going to the common room as he usually did, he went straight out and did it. So he wasn't drunk, and he wasn't drugged.

ANNE: Did you see him yesterday?

MERVYN: Yes. The last thing he was at was the English seminar.

ANNE: Your seminar.

MERVYN: Yes.

ANNE: Did anything happen?

MERVYN: No.

ANNE: How did he seem?

MERVYN: As usual. He asked his usual damnfool questions.

ANNE: What about?

MERVYN: Oh, what does it matter? He never got any answers. I don't think he expected any. I don't think there are any. I think that's why he asked them. Awkward bugger. With your normal student, if he's doing English Literature he does English Literature, if he's doing philosophy he does philosophy — he doesn't want bloody connections all the time, bloody relevances . . . I remember once when *I* was at school, one of the other kids said to the Maths teacher, "Sir, I don't see the point in Algebra; what's it for?" The teacher said, "What it's for is for doing in my

class; and why you do it is because I tell you. Now
do it.'' I thought that was a good answer.

ANNE: Did you?

MERVYN: Well — it simplifies things. He was
obsessed with the minor Victorian poets, can you
believe it?

ANNE: Simpson?

MERVYN: Perhaps he identified. He wrote poetry.

ANNE: Any good?

MERVYN: I don't think so. Those young late-
Victorian layabouts, the Tragic Generation
somebody called them: Lord Alfred Douglas and
Dowson and Symons and the rest; commuting
between London and Paris on a pittance; a slim
volume of mediocre verse, wispy stuff, what one
of my lecturers used to call ''romanticism strained
through a silk stocking''; much discussion of Art
and a few fucked chorus girls, that was their life.

ANNE: You get very reactionary when you're
upset.

MERVYN: I wouldn't think you'd have much
sympathy with that lot, do you?

ANNE: They don't bother me.

MERVYN: His sixty-four dollar question this time
was, ''Which is more valuable, a poet's life or his
poetry?'' I said, ''Valuable to whom?'' He said,
''Do you mean value is subjective?'' I said, ''Of
course it is, or there'd be no-one to evaluate it.''
He said, ''I was reading some Ernest Dowson. He
had a wretched life, he died at thirty-two, and he
left one or two good poems.'' He said, ''Do you
think it would have been better if he'd lived a
contented life and not written any poetry?'' I said,
''*I* think not, obviously, because he's dead and his
poetry is still around.'' Then he said, ''So you do
value poetry higher than life.'' I said, ''I don't
think I said that. Now do you think we could get
back to literature and leave the metaphysics

for some other time?'' He said, ''Yes, all right.''
And walked out.

ANNE: Oh . . . What was it, a cry for help?

MERVYN: Oh, don't be fatuous.

ANNE: Or a suicide note.

MERVYN: Maybe it *was* an accident. That's what
his father wants to believe.

ANNE: Did you tell the father about the seminar?

MERVYN: No, of course not. It probably had
nothing to do with it. He was always trying to be
profound. Bloody pseud. If it was a cry for help
he was asking rather a lot. Anyway, he's stopped
asking now.

Anne looks sharply at him

I've still got a book he lent me. He kept asking if
I'd read it. I don't know whether to give it back.

ANNE: I wouldn't.

MERVYN: Darling, I've got something else to tell
you.

Anne freezes

David and Helen are back in England. I've invited
them to a meal on Saturday. Is that all right?

HELEN: The first thing I felt was anger at myself. It
was so obvious. I thought back. It was so obvious.
What a fool I was. What a fool they must take me
for. And how many others knew? Mervyn, surely,
or is he as big a fool as me? Then at them, the
anger: my husband, to take my best friend; my
best friend, to take my husband. How could they?
To betray me, so thoughtlessly, so blatantly. It
was vile. And for what? To fuck one another. To
fuck one another they'd betray me, betray
Mervyn, betray the friendship. What was it, to
make them do that? What did they have, what did

they get to pay for it? What was it they had
together to do that for? Then the self-pity: I was
betrayed, I was rejected, I had no-one, I was
nothing, there was no-one I could trust, there was
no trust, there was no value. There was nothing
but getting what you wanted; nothing else. Then
the revenge. I'll have *him*. I'll have him, I'll have
hers.

MERVYN: Back of the hand barely touching the
skirt. God, I thought, they must feel it back there,
the waves of it, like bloody D-Day! After that it
was torment. Of course it was totally impossible:
her best friend, the wife of my best friend; we
lived practically in each other's pockets. It was
mad. I tried to rationalize it away. I said: It's
obvious what's happened. She's rather fallen for
me for some reason, after all this time, perhaps
they're having trouble; she's dissatisfied, looking
around for something else. But that's her
business. I don't have to follow suit. I'm flattered,
that's all it is, because she wants me at a time when
I don't feel particularly wanted. Don't be a fool,
don't behave like a child. Keep clear. Forget it.
It'll go away. I knew the cost of it, I was no
beginner: the sick excitement, the lurchings, the
constant planning, the tearing in two; a few
islands of extraordinary happiness in a waste of
messy discomfort. I've wondered since whether I
could have stood out against it. I don't know, I
suppose I could, I was a rational human being,
part of me anyway. The letting go is always a
conscious decision, whatever they say. What
tipped the balance, as before, as always, was first,
an anger. How dare things be this way! That the
simple, good coming together of two people is
made an act of madness! Then a fear. I was afraid
of losing something of myself, afraid, in a way, of
dying. The need, the desire, whatever it was, was

my experience; it was real, however painful it was, however perverse, it was mine, it was me, it was the only real thing about me, that awful obsessive clawing, the clawing of that need to be myself, to do what needed to be done if I were not to kill part of myself by killing that need. So I did it; or it was done. One day I let go.

DAVID: By the way, Mervyn rang while you were out.

HELEN: Oh, did he?

DAVID: I said we'd be there. Eight o'clock.

HELEN: Good . . .

DAVID: He didn't recognize my voice; he thought he'd got the wrong number.

HELEN: Your voice has softened.

DAVID: Have you noticed that?

HELEN: Oh yes . . . Did he say anything?

DAVID: They're both quite well. He *is* a head teacher now. So of course he's not doing much teaching.

HELEN: That seems a pity. I imagine he was a good teacher.

DAVID: He'd have used a lot of energy. It's not necessarily the same thing.

HELEN: I know it's not. I said I imagine he was a good teacher.

DAVID: Yes, I expect he was. Then he asked how we were . . .

HELEN: Did you tell him?

DAVID: What?

HELEN: How we are.

DAVID: You mean about the therapy?

HELEN: Yes.

DAVID: Yes, I told him about that. You don't mind, do you?

HELEN: No, of course not.

DAVID: I didn't go into details.

HELEN: It doesn't matter. They'll see we've

changed. You like people to know, don't
you?

DAVID: I don't see any point in keeping it secret.

HELEN: I mean you like to talk about it. You like
to tell people how well you are.

DAVID: I don't boast about it.

HELEN: No.

DAVID: Odd coincidence. When I mentioned the
therapy he said he'd been lent the book.

HELEN: Has he read it?

DAVID: I think so.

HELEN: We'll have something to live up to.

DAVID: You're not worried about seeing them, are
you?

HELEN: It'll be strange. They'll be the same people
they were. They'll expect us to be. It'll be like
meeting our old selves again. I wonder why they
want to see us.

DAVID: Friendship . . .

HELEN: I'm not so sure of myself as you are. I
don't want to hurt them and I don't want to be
hurt. It'll upset me if they're in a mess. It'll still
upset me. I'm not that cured. You want to show
them how well you've come out of it, don't you?
How sane you are; how balanced.

DAVID: I don't think so.

HELEN: Why do you want to go then? They've got
nothing to give us. They'll just remind us.

DAVID: We should be able to face that. I think
you're making too much of it. It'll be a pleasant
evening.

HELEN: I suppose you're right. A touch of the old
sinking feeling; something unresolved somewhere.
We'll either enjoy it or not enjoy it. There's
nothing else, is there?

ANNE: The beauty of it; my God, the beauty of it;
when we first made it. All that need, all the
accumulated energy of that need for him, which

had been like a sickness, suddenly to be used, used, used . . . Only, afterwards, a day or two later, the need was there again. And now there were two things: the need again, and the memory of what it was like to lose it. And still I'd die, still my time was passing, it didn't stop that, just increased the urgency of it. I'd count the times, count the weeks that passed, live weeks or dead weeks: a live week, with him in it, a dead week without. I watched over my time like an accountant, the losses and gains, the wastage, the profit. The balance was always out, they all became dead weeks — they were all lost when I'd had them, good or bad; they left nothing, nothing but the need and the desire, nothing but more evidence of the only time I had passing, time dying, leaving need, more need. I grew voracious. I hunted my time like a wild animal, tore at it, wolfed it down. One evening, I came back from David, Mervyn was in bed, reading; I fell on him, tore love from him.

HELEN: Rather like an old film I've seen before. I still run it now and then, like an old home movie, run it through my mind, for amusement or — some reason; not from necessity, the obsession is gone. I watch the antics of the participants, their funny goings on, watch their mouths turn up and down, open and close . . . A nearly silent film, most of the words are gone, a few shreds come back — *(She looks upward)* — not possible, we shall have to — out of the house you cow . . . Oh God do that oh God do that oh God do that oh God . . . *(She laughs)* Rushes from an abandoned B-movie. And through it all the mouths open and close; all those words, so serious, so heartfelt, all those lies, all that desperate honesty, trying to explain, trying to understand, trying to justify; all gone, wiped off. Together with whatever powered

it, the engine of it. Just a recollection left of pain
and delight; it seemed to be all pain and delight;
and the two, from here, oddly similar . . .

MERVYN: Simpson's father rang again today. I met
him for a drink on the way home.

ANNE: I wondered why you were late.

MERVYN: I tried to ring. You were engaged.

ANNE: What did he want?

MERVYN: To talk. So I let him.

ANNE: Did it help?

MERVYN: I don't know.

ANNE: What does he do?

MERVYN: Some sort of business man. He has to
make a decision about his son.

ANNE: What?

MERVYN: They want to switch off the machine. I
asked him to let me know.

ANNE: Why?

MERVYN: I don't know . . . I rang David today, by
the way.

ANNE: Oh?

MERVYN: They *are* coming on Saturday, I said
eight o'clock.

ANNE: Right.

MERVYN: That's all right, is it?

ANNE: You've done it now, haven't you?

MERVYN: You think it's a mistake? You only have
to say so. Sometimes you make me feel like a
schoolboy waiting outside the headmaster's study.

ANNE: You *are* the headmaster. You're in charge.

MERVYN: It doesn't feel like it to me. I was always
terrified of authority figures, and now I am one it
doesn't make any difference. I tell you, I spend
most of my energy at school hiding that dark
secret from everyone, kids and staff — that under
this forbidding exterior there's a quivering schoolboy, waiting eternally outside the head's study.
That's why I come home so tired, I'm not in

charge, I don't know who the hell is, but it's not
me. At least at home I don't have to pretend it is.

ANNE: It's certainly not me.

MERVYN: Maybe no-one is. We're up shit creek in
a barbed wire canoe without a captain.

ANNE: So you're disclaiming responsibility.

MERVYN: For what?

ANNE: Whatever you think I'm upset about.
Whatever you feel guilty about.

MERVYN: Is that what I'm doing?

ANNE: As usual. You've always done that; said
you were not responsible — in some vague way I
can't argue against.

MERVYN: So I'm unoriginal. Don't throw my guilt
at me. That *is* the dirty trick. I have guilt whether
I'm guilty or not. I'm built on guilt. Guilt-built.
You know that.

ANNE: You did it over her.

MERVYN: What?

ANNE: Is that what it is? You're so guilt-stricken
you have to find things to use it up on? You did
the same thing over her. ''You can't blame me,
I'm not responsible for my actions.''

MERVYN: I never said that.

ANNE: The destruction caused in this world by
people who act in spite of themselves.

MERVYN: You're not blameless, are you?

ANNE: Where I'm not blameless I take the blame.
That's the difference.

MERVYN: I never said I wasn't responsible.

ANNE: Not so simply.

MERVYN: There's a difference between taking
responsibility for one's actions and being able to
change them.

ANNE: What?

MERVYN: I mean I was *impelled* . . .

ANNE: You couldn't help yourself.

MERVYN: Not that, not that! I mean . . . What I

mean is, I wish you'd listen to me. What I mean is,
being the kind of man I am, I can't find it in
myself to — cancel out that impulse, to kill it,
even if I could, I don't know whether I could, but
even if I could . . . But I still — though I can't
help the kind of man I am, was — feel I must take
— responsibility for what I do. You see, it's not
that simple.

ANNE: And do it all the same.

MERVYN: If I can stand it, yes, I'm afraid, if I can
stand the consequences, yes.

ANNE: Good for you.

MERVYN: Which, I may say for your reassurance,
takes more stamina than I have any more, more —
more something . . .

ANNE: Libido?

MERVYN: Don't give me that psychoanalytical shit.

ANNE: You prefer to wrap it up in your own
special jargon, don't you, so it seems to have some
sort of value? As if you're doing mankind a
favour, leading it to greater heights. Instead of
just saying: I wanted to have it off, so I had it off.

MERVYN: Is that how you thought of you and
David?

ANNE: How else?

MERVYN: I don't believe you.

ANNE: Please yourself.

Pause

MERVYN: I wish to God I hadn't invited them now.

ANNE: It's a bit late to say that. So it's just your
lack of stamina that's stopping you now? Are you
getting past it at last?

MERVYN: I didn't say it was just my lack of
stamina.

ANNE: Sorry, I thought you did. If you were a little
less convoluted perhaps we'd understand each
other better.

MERVYN: Life isn't simple.

ANNE: You can say that again. Why *did* you invite them?

MERVYN: I heard they were back in England so I rang them, that's all.

ANNE: Without letting me know.

MERVYN: I did let you know.

ANNE: After you'd arranged it.

MERVYN: I could have put them off today if you'd told me you didn't want to see them.

ANNE: What? "I'm sorry, but Anne doesn't want to see you"?

MERVYN: It was an impulse. I rang them on the spur of the moment. I do that little enough nowadays. God knows.

ANNE: Did you have their number?

MERVYN: I knew they were living in Esher. So I rang directory enquiries.

ANNE: From school. All on an impulse.

MERVYN: Anyway, if I'd mentioned it first you'd have put it off. You'd have said, "Oh, later, later." We'd never have seen them.

ANNE: Now we're getting to it. You are a devious bugger. You've got some purpose in mind; you're up to something, aren't you?

MERVYN: All I've done is invite a couple of friends round for the evening.

ANNE: They're not friends. One thing necessary for friendship is communication, and we haven't communicated for years.

MERVYN: We send Christmas cards to each other. We never actually fell out with them.

ANNE: Don't be naïve. And you're so bad at being devious. It always shows. It always did. That forced casualness, the hooded look in the eyes. You don't know how transparent you are.

MERVYN: That's *my* misfortune.

ANNE: Mine.

MERVYN: Whereas you can deceive me and I know nothing about it.

ANNE: Deceive you? Where? When? What are you talking about? I haven't deceived you for years.

MERVYN: Nor I you.

ANNE: I know you haven't. I don't need telling. When I deceive I do it properly.

MERVYN: When you tell me you do it properly too, don't you?

ANNE: Oh God, we're not going over all this again, are we? Why do you have to rake it all up?

MERVYN: I'm not raking it up. It's there already, it's there all the time, you know that. You want to write it all off, don't you, pretend it didn't really happen, have nothing more to do with it? I can't do that if you can.

ANNE: I'm not asking you to. Just keep it to yourself.

MERVYN: You want us to behave as if we'd never met them.

ANNE: I wish to God we hadn't.

MERVYN: Everything would have been all right then, wouldn't it? Everything would have gone swimmingly, if we'd just not met them.

ANNE: Oh, I don't know . . . I just don't want to think about it. Sometimes I feel like a clockwork toy that's been wound up and set in a particular direction and off I've gone on my clockwork legs. When I think of the time and energy I've spent trying to change things, trying to sort things out, it just makes me angry. Wasted effort. I might just as well let things happen, they do anyway. I don't want to be reminded of all that wasted effort. I don't know why you want reminding of it.

MERVYN: I don't like unfinished things.

ANNE: You think it's not finished?

MERVYN: Nothing ever finished. There was an explosion; nothing finished, nothing was resolved.

ANNE: So what do you expect to happen on Saturday?

MERVYN: I don't know.

ANNE: Right.

MERVYN: Strange thing. You know this book Simpson lent me?

ANNE: No.

MERVYN: I told you. It's about a new type of psychotherapy that's going in the States. And David and Helen have had it.

ANNE: Both of them?

MERVYN: Mm.

ANNE: Why did he tell you that?

MERVYN: He happened to mention it.

ANNE: People don't normally tell all and sundry they've been in analysis, do they?

MERVYN: It's not analysis. It's quite different. I've read the book.

ANNE: I just wondered if they're blaming us for it.

MERVYN: He didn't *put* it like that. Apparently he had a complete breakdown.

ANNE: When?

MERVYN: A few years ago.

ANNE: Has it done them any good, this therapy?

MERVYN: He says it has.

ANNE: Bully for them.

MERVYN: He talked about being cured.

ANNE: What of? Us?

MERVYN: We were probably just a symptom.

ANNE: Delightful.

DAVID: It became impossible. After the break-up, the change of partners, the break-up again, the reunion — all terribly serious, as if it were something of significance — after that we got the hell out. I had a chance in the States, we honestly thought we could start again. Dishonestly thought. "Let's make a fresh start, leave the past behind us." That's how we might have put it,

following the old pattern. It couldn't work, of
course, we carried our old selves with us, on our
backs. Carried each other. We pussy-footed
around for a time, being terribly gentle with each
other, very courteous and polite and considerate;
as if we were leading each other across water
covered with very thin ice. Yes, that's the way it
was: we crept about gingerly, pretending not to
notice that under our feet the ice creaked. And
then, for me, gave way. And I was in. That was
the end of the pretence that we lived in a solid
world. It was like going into icy water; first the
awful humiliating shock of giving way, going in
headlong, thrashing about; then the acceptance,
that I was engulfed in this new medium, no
question of escape, no toeholds, no fingerholds;
I gave myself up, with relief, to drowning. But
they pulled me out, laid me in white in an anti-
septic environment, some place or other. The firm
paid, with bad grace, I think; but they honoured
their obligations — written in; brought me to dry
land, put me carefully back in the swim — *(with
a little laugh)* — in the shallows, where I'd do no
harm. I knew they'd never promote me, of course,
not after going through the ice. My limits were set;
I might survive, with care. We lived timidly again,
looking after each other, aware of the water
swirling about underneath, the ice creaking. Then
I read about the method; the therapy. It was
supposed to work; well, we had nothing to lose.
MERVYN: Came the time when I realized Anne
knew; and a new ritual set in. Having to make
excuses for absence, knowing they weren't
believed: "Stopped for a drink on the way, met
so-and-so" — knowing she knew I lied. But the
game had to be played out. "Oh, how is he? What
did he say?" "Fine, I think. Nothing of interest.
Sends his regards." She knew; I knew she knew;

she knew I knew she knew. We played the game,
terrified of what would happen if it came into the
open. And taking it with me when I went to see her
— Helen. Taking, I mean, Anne's — suffering. I
tried not to call it that, but there was no other
word for it. Suffering. Her suffering which I
caused. Did I stop? No; I went on: more, it drove
me from the house, I tried to escape from it, if it
was only for an hour or two. Made love to *her*;
and it was beautiful, beautiful. And all the time,
her suffering, inside me, clawing. Till it broke.

DAVID: Seven o'clock.

HELEN: We're not going yet, surely?

DAVID: It's seven now. It'll take an hour.

HELEN: I don't want to get there too early. They'll
only ply us with drinks, you know how it is.

DAVID: You can always refuse.

HELEN: I don't like refusing. If people offer me
things in good heart, I don't like to keep saying
no. It's different for you.

DAVID: How?

HELEN: You don't mind. It quite pleases you:
showing how little you need; compared with other
people.

DAVID: You think I'm smug about it? I don't think
so. I'm glad to feel good, I suppose I show it.
There's nothing wrong with that.

HELEN: Do you remember the Mexican holiday?
Coming out of the hotel complex, all shade trees
and fountains and waiters carrying trays of
drinks, not even any flies, they must have sprayed
it at night, while we were asleep in our air-
conditioned room; and just outside, the dusty
road and the beggars?

DAVID: Professional beggars.

HELEN: Professional or amateur, they hadn't
enough to eat. We had, we had more than enough.

DAVID: We gave them money.

HELEN: I know we did; till they recognized us, saw us coming. I'm not talking about what we could do about it, I'm talking about how I felt: as if I were somehow flaunting my good fortune — which is all it is; not virtue; we're no *better* than them, only better off. I wanted to be invisible going out of that gate. I used to put a straight face on, try not to look happy.

DAVID: What good does that do?

HELEN: None. None. Nothing does any good. Except going there on holiday, I suppose, spending as much as we can there, some of the money must filter back to the ones at the bottom of the heap.

DAVID: It's rather illogical to get upset over things you can't do anything about.

HELEN: I know.

DAVID: We'd better go to Sweden this year.

HELEN: Mm.

DAVID: I don't see what this has to do with going to see Mervyn and Anne.

HELEN: I'm just a little apprehensive.

DAVID: What are you afraid of? Say it.

HELEN: I'm afraid that at some point tonight — of course it won't happen — at some point Mervyn or Anne might say: What value do you put on what happened, between the four of us, or between any two of us? What was its meaning, what was its significance; what has it left, what was it worth? And I'd have to answer, if I were honest: Nothing. There was no meaning to it, it had no significance, unless you like to say it signified a sickness I'm now cured of; it had no value — except to show how sick we were and you, perhaps, still are; it's left nothing but regret now and then that, now and then, it comes back into my mind. The past was not just unpleasant, more unpleasant than we knew at the time, but meaningless; without meaning. If it could all have been avoided it would have been better.

DAVID: Not better . . .

HELEN: No, not even that. It would have been neither more nor less meaningful. If it had never happened.

DAVID: Then why say it? You're not obliged to be honest.

HELEN: It's true, though, isn't it? It's all the same whether it happened or not.

DAVID: Except that you could say it pushed us into getting some help for ourselves. Getting the therapy. That gives it point, doesn't it?

HELEN: So the only point of pain is to make us want to relieve it.

DAVID: What else?

HELEN: Nothing. Nothing.

DAVID: The present is all we have to live in. That's meaning enough, surely?

HELEN: Yes . . . All the same, I hope they don't ask the question.

DAVID: They're not likely to.

MERVYN: One evening she confronted me with it. Both sitting quietly after supper, with our books — no, reading essays, I was; "Discuss the proposition; poetry is unnecessary." Suddenly she said, "You're having an affair with Helen, aren't you?" I looked up; she seemed to be still engrossed in her book; our little carriage clock ticked away on the mantelpiece; a peaceful scene, domestic relaxation after the rigours of the day. "Yes," I said; no hesitation, no decision made; a casual answer to a casual question. She sat there still, nothing happened. I suddenly felt as if all the mess had gone out of it, all the deception, only the clean, pure, simple facts were left. There was no need to hide anything any more. Things were as they were, neither good nor bad; we had

somehow cleansed the situation. A plane went
over; it was the summer season, tourists were
going to sunny places for their package fortnights
away from it all. A cartoon came into my mind —
Steinberg, I think — of an aircraft full of
passengers, only he'd left the aircraft undrawn:
four rows of well-dressed people sat calmly in
mid-air, waiting to arrive. She was still sitting
there but not reading. Her hand was across her
mouth and she was staring at me. Then the
questions: where, when, for how long, what did
you do; what do you want to happen; very cool
and calm. Cool and calm like the boffin on the
beach, carefully unscrewing the detonator from
the new kind of mine. Then she said: You know,
do you, I've been having it away with David; for
some time now; very good it was; is. Better than
you.

ANNE: I asked questions; he answered them; very
civilized, I said: What do you want to happen
now? He said: What I *want* is to go on with it, and
not hurt you. That's what I *want*. I said: All right.
You know, do you, I'm having a big thing with
David; have been, for some time.

MERVYN: Nothing happened then. It seemed even
simpler, even straighter: she with David, Helen
with me; still the foursome, still friends, no-one
left out, only something added; what could be
neater? What more logical?

ANNE: Which you've ruined for me, of course. For
years you had your women; now when I have my
chance you ruin it for me; you realize that.

MERVYN: When it hit it hit hard and sudden.
Below the belt, between the eyes; it was a
knockout. I was mad, as near as makes no
difference; possessed. I swore at her, pried for
details, more and more details, which she
supplied; was obscene, was violent. And even

while she still crouched on the floor, while I still
stood over her, after I'd hit her, and hit her, and
hit her, I knew the justification was only in my
fists. There was no logic; logic was gone. She did
what I did. The value of my affair was the value of
hers. The obsceneness of hers was the obsceneness
of mine. The truth was the same as the lie, the
beauty was the same as the ugliness. Everything
was its opposite; there was no fixed point, no
truth, no rightness, no logic. It was all, totally,
meaningless.

ANNE: Are you going to change?

MERVYN: Do you think I need to?

ANNE: I don't know what you need. I don't know
what you want.

MERVYN: What do you mean?

ANNE: I don't know whether you want to look
your best or look your old self. It's up to you. I
don't know why you invited them, I don't know
why they're coming, I don't know how I'm
supposed to behave, I don't know anything. Don't
ask me whether you need to change.

MERVYN: Right. What are we eating?

ANNE: Oxtail.

MERVYN: Ah.

ANNE: I thought a bit of tail might be appropriate.

MERVYN: Devilled relationships to follow?

ANNE: Hm. So you're not changing.

MERVYN: No.

ANNE: The old self look. Are you going to be
pissed when they arrive? Or will you wait till later?

MERVYN: It's only my second.

ANNE: Your second what, quadruple?

MERVYN: There's another bottle.

ANNE: That's all right then. We can all get pissed.

MERVYN: To look my old self I'd need a face job.

ANNE: I'm surprised you didn't think of that. I
wonder what we'll talk about? The kids, how

they've grown up, what they're doing now; how
did you find the United States? I do love the way
you cook oxtail, you must give me the recipe. It's
been so nice seeing you again. We did enjoy it, you
must come and visit us, it'll be just like old times.
Do you think we could possibly have a normal,
sociable evening . . .? I do want to see them. I
really do.

MERVYN: I know you do, or you would have
stopped it.

ANNE: It's just that I'm terrified.

MERVYN: What of?

ANNE: I don't know. The past.

MERVYN: This isn't the past, it's the present.

ANNE: Don't be facile.

MERVYN: There's nothing to worry about.

ANNE: Not with a bellyful of Scotch.

MERVYN: Have some, then.

ANNE: I think I'd better. Are you going to put that
book away before they arrive?

MERVYN: What for?

ANNE: It'll look rather pointed, won't it? Reading
about their treatment.

MERVYN: I told David I'd got it. I don't think
they're embarrassed about it.

ANNE: Have you finished it?

MERVYN: Yes.

ANNE: Well?

MERVYN: It sounds very good. Very convincing. It
makes sense.

ANNE: Do you think it works?

MERVYN: Yes, I do. I have the feeling it does. With
the right people anyway. There's a lot of case
histories, autobiographical bits. You get rid of
your hangups; live totally in the present. They say
it's marvellous.

ANNE: Well, that's good.

MERVYN: Yes . . .

The telephone rings. Mervyn takes it

Hallo . . . Oh, yes . . . Tonight . . . I see . . . Well
. . . Yes, of course; of course you have. Thank you
for letting me know . . . Yes, we must . . .
Good-bye. *(He puts the receiver down)* That was
Simpson senior. They're switching him off
tonight.

HELEN: After we got to the States I slept a lot;
every spare minute. We must have seemed a rather
dull couple, staying home evenings, polite but
unresponsive to neighbours, watching TV, being
nice to each other; I wondered whether they took
us for a typical English couple. One afternoon a
neighbour called in to borrow some shortening, to
make a few cookies for the kiddies. I offered her
a cup of tea, we sat drinking it. Suddenly she said:
Is there anything wrong? Is there anything I can
do? Her eyes were full of concern. I wonder what
she would have done if I'd told her: Well, you see,
my husband fell in love with a great friend of mine
and was having an affair with her, so I fell in love
with the husband, since he was a great friend of
my husband, and I was having an affair with him;
but we couldn't stand that, so my friend's
husband, that is my lover, left his wife, and I went
off and lived with him for a while, leaving the
other two to more or less live with each other as
well; but this didn't work either, so I'm back with
my husband and she's back with hers. Which
sounds fine on the face of it, an interesting
experiment in alternative living, except that on the
way a few things got lost. I don't believe in love
any more, for instance, or trust, or fidelity, or the
sanctity of anything at all, or truth, or value, or,
I'm afraid, meaning; meaning I don't believe in.
I don't even believe in the innocent concern in
those wide blue Country-and-Western eyes,

Mrs Levington, with your nice comfy hubby who
calls you honey and your kiddies and your
cookies. I don't believe the world you live in is any
more solid than mine. You've just been lucky so
far. But I didn't say that. I simply, suddenly,
cried. And cried. And cried . . . But then we found
the therapy. And after a while, everything was
fine. I've never felt better. I wonder what I ever
bothered about.

DAVID: Time to go?
HELEN: Yes.

A door bell rings

ANNE: That sounds like them.
MERVYN: Shall I go?
ANNE: Let's both go.

END OF ACT ONE

ACT TWO

(The living-room of Anne and Mervyn.

The telephone is ringing. Mervyn, a glass of whisky in his hand, enters to answer it)

MERVYN: Hallo . . . Yes, I rang earlier, you were to ring back, was it you I spoke to? . . . Yes . . . I see. Well, no, I don't. Did Matron give any reason why I shouldn't be told? . . . She doesn't have to know, does she? . . . Yes, of course, I understand, I expressed myself badly. What I meant was, she's probably very busy and doesn't want to be bothered with . . . There's no definite rule against, is there? . . . I told you, I was his headmaster. And I'm a friend of his father. Well, you know, he may not feel like ringing people up afterwards . . . No, no good reason. I'd just like to know when it's been done. It just happens to be — emotionally important to me . . . Yes . . . Yes, of course, only when you have a moment . . . That's so good of you, I do appreciate it, I know how busy you must be . . . Thank you so much. Good-bye. *(He puts down the receiver, finishes his drink, and pours another)*

Helen, Anne and David enter. Anne has a coffee tray which she puts on the coffee-table.

DAVID: You can't save energy by making life more complex. That's the real law of conservation.
HELEN: Anne wants to know the answer, David.
DAVID: It's a false problem.
ANNE: Conservation isn't important?
DAVID: I mean we state the problem wrongly. It's ourselves we have to conserve, our nervous energies. Do that and the natural resources will take care of themselves.

ANNE: I don't know what you're talking about.

DAVID: I'm saying change people, not things. It's people use the energy, not things. Don't you see?

ANNE: No, honestly.

MERVYN: Make yourselves comfortable, folks. *(Indicating a chair)* Helen, sit there.

HELEN: Why?

MERVYN: I don't know — so I can look at you. I don't want to look at him, do I?

They sit

ANNE: Helen, would you like some more coffee?

HELEN: Thanks, Anne, I've had plenty.

ANNE: David?

DAVID: I'm fine, thanks.

ANNE: Where's your cup?

MERVYN: Buggered if I know. There, on the table. *(He brings it over)*

ANNE: Was that the hospital?

MERVYN: Yes. Had to shine my charm on the little nurse. She said the Matron wouldn't like it. I said the Matron's not going to get it, dear. Bloody ridiculous.

ANNE: I don't know why you want to know, it doesn't make any difference.

MERVYN: Anyway, she's going to let me know. *(To the others)* Pupil of mine. In hospital. Well — here we all are.

ANNE: You're sure you won't have more coffee, there's plenty?

HELEN: No, thanks.

DAVID: I'm fine as I am.

HELEN: It was a lovely meal.

ANNE: It did turn out well, didn't it?

DAVID: Delicious. I do enjoy my food nowadays.

MERVYN: You always did as I remember. You've lost a bit of weight, haven't you? Don't you think so, darling?

DAVID: I eat less and enjoy it more.

HELEN: He's given up the big fat business lunches.

DAVID: Do you know, for years I stuffed myself with food every lunchtime, you know the kind of thing, taking a couple of clients to the little place I know. "Hallo, Luigi, what have you got for us today?" Luigi all smarms, playing the game as hard as we did. Campari to start, brandy to finish, forgoing the sweet as if we were making a sacrifice; very jolly and important, business, you see; make friends and you make business, the firm's motto. It was a game; no business was done, we weren't such fools. One day I woke up to the fact that I hate big meals in the middle of the day, I don't *like* lunches; not under those conditions, anyway. I'd been fooling myself. I stopped it. I do just as well; or if I don't it doesn't worry me. It's not a price I'd pay any more.

MERVYN: What opened your eyes?

DAVID: The treatment.

MERVYN: The therapy.

DAVID: Yes.

MERVYN: Uhuh.

DAVID: You haven't asked me about it.

MERVYN: I shall.

HELEN: Do you remember we were always dragging you out to some new little place he'd discovered? The walking good-food-guide.

DAVID: Don't embarrass me.

MERVYN: We enjoyed it; you made our decisions for us, it was like having a nanny to look after us.

ANNE: Once you made me send my plate back to the kitchen. You insisted it was the wrong colour or something. Can't let them get away with that, you said; I had to have something else, and I was dying for that dish.

DAVID: I must have been unbearable.

MERVYN: No, it was part of you, part of your character. It endeared you to us.

DAVID: Yet the one thing I never did was really taste the food. It was all theoretical. I didn't really *taste* it.

MERVYN: You fooled me.

DAVID: I fooled myself. There was a case of a man who always had charcoal-grilled steak. He had the therapy and found he hated the taste of charcoal-grilled steak. He'd always hated it.

MERVYN: Yes, I read about that.

ANNE: So why did he have it?

DAVID: He thought it was part of the good life. I spent my time fooling myself, one way and another. Having what I didn't really want, then sweating to pay for it. That's what I was talking about, Anne. I was consuming energy not to enjoy the product but to placate an inner need, a monster inside, a parasite. We sweat ourselves silly, deplete the earth, to feed that parasite, and it's all a waste of time; because the need is really a need for love, childhood love; which you can never give it, because childhood is over. What a substitute for love, eh, charcoal-grilled steaks.

Pause

MERVYN: Symbolic though.

Slight pause

DAVID: Then there were the gadgets.

HELEN: Don't keep on about it, David.

DAVID: Sorry, am I boring you?

ANNE: No.

MERVYN: We'll let you know.

DAVID: You remember those gadgets I was always bringing home? Electric potato-peelers . . .

ANNE: What's wrong with electric potato-peelers?

MERVYN: That's it, David, you talk and my wife

will supply the feed-lines. What's wrong with
electric potato-peelers, apart from the difficulty of
getting electric potatoes?

HELEN: David objects to *dishwashers*.

ANNE: Haven't you got one?

HELEN: Yes, but he objects to it.

DAVID: I object to the *idea* of the *necessity* of a
dishwasher. *(To Helen)* You know what I'm
talking about.

ANNE: *I* object to the idea of washing up.

DAVID: *(showing his hands)* These are dishwashers.

ANNE: *(indicating herself and Helen)* No, David,
these are dishwashers.

HELEN: He's not really an M.C.P.

ANNE: Sounds a bit piggy to me. I bet you don't
object to labour-saving devices in your office.
Including your secretary.

DAVID: I do object to my secretary as a matter of
fact. She's a bad secretary.

ANNE: Doesn't she do what you tell her?

DAVID: She *only* does what I tell her.

MERVYN: Lovely.

DAVID: Like a dishwasher. Like a machine.
There's no joy in machines.

ANNE: There's no joy in washing up.

DAVID: There *can* be. There *should* be.

ANNE: Go and do it then. It's all out there.

DAVID: You've got a dishwasher, haven't you?

ANNE: Oh, *David* . . .

HELEN: You're being just a tiny bit inconsistent,
David.

DAVID: No, I'm not. We live in the world we live
in, I'll grant you that . . .

MERVYN: Very magnanimous of you.

DAVID: If a dishwasher's there and there's
something you'd rather be doing you use it.

ANNE: Which I would.

DAVID: All I'm objecting to — not objecting, I think it's sad — is that we've come to the point where we don't like doing *anything*. We can't even clean our teeth any more, we have some electrical gadget to do it for us. We don't want to live, it bores us, we want machines to take over.

ANNE: Who's we?

DAVID: All right, I'm generalizing; but it's true.

MERVYN: Vibrators.

DAVID: Exactly.

MERVYN: What a quaint old-fashioned chap you are.

DAVID: Not at all, I don't object to machinery *per se*.

ANNE: Then what are you on about?

DAVID: I'm on about something very serious actually. Perversion, the true perversion: living outside the body, which is all we really *have* to live with; living in machines; living in philosophy; living in politics; living in art . . .

Pause

MERVYN: How's the painting going?

ANNE: Yes, I meant to ask.

DAVID: Oh, I've stopped.

ANNE: Given it up?

DAVID: Yes. Some time ago.

ANNE: Why?

DAVID: I lost interest; just didn't want to paint any more. I never really enjoyed it.

ANNE: Then why *did* you paint?

DAVID: Oh — for something to do . . .

ANNE: Oh, come on . . .

DAVID: I couldn't bear not to be active, producing something. It was all part of the sickness. And for — esteem; it made me feel important. I wanted to be talented.

HELEN: You were.

DAVID: Well, maybe I was; but at what?

HELEN: You could express yourself . . .

DAVID: Express what? My hang-ups: my sickness;
my need. I found some the other day, some
drawings I'd forgotten about. Those tortured
figures! The futility of it. A sick man drawing his
sickness. Who for? What for?

HELEN: Then he put them in the dustbin.

ANNE: What sort of a gesture was that?

DAVID: It wasn't a gesture. I didn't want them.
They were of no interest.

Pause

HELEN: How are you both?

MERVYN: *Apropos* tortured figures?

HELEN: No . . .

MERVYN: What a question to suddenly spring. All
right, I'll stick my neck out: we're well, I suppose.
Are we, dear heart?

ANNE: Yes, we're splendid

MERVYN: There you are, we're splendid. Keeping
our heads above water, in other words, while
soldiering on through shot and shell. And how are
you?

HELEN: I'm very well, thank you.

MERVYN: Don't thank me. You look well. As for
you, David, my old mate, you're like a cat in front
of the fire, a picture of self-satisfaction.

DAVID: Do you mean smug?

MERVYN: I didn't say that.

DAVID: I feel fine actually. Really fine.

MERVYN: That's good.

ANNE: It is good to see you both. I was nervous,
you know. I mean at the thought of seeing you
again after so long . . . I mean people change, you
know? Silly really — I mean, to worry . . .

MERVYN: I mean . . .

ANNE: Would you like some brandy!

HELEN: No, I'm all right as I am, thanks.

ANNE: For you, David?

DAVID: I'm fine.

ANNE: I know you're fine, but do you want some brandy?

DAVID: I won't, thanks.

ANNE: Darling?

MERVYN: I'll stick to whisky. Some for you?

ANNE: I might as well.

MERVYN: Darling, don't say you might as well, not with whisky, not at four quid a bottle. All the time she says she might as well. She goes through life like a depressed housewife in a supermarket: hand poised over the shelves, hypnotized by an infinity of choices, between almost identical products, all mediocre. Which shall it be? Gravity takes over, the hand falls, on a packet of Vesta curry. Might as well. She said it in bed the other day.

ANNE: And who are you, Jean-Paul Sartre or somebody?

MERVYN: Why don't you say "Yes" to life? Or "No" to life. You can't say "I might as well" to life. Well, not to whisky. If you might as well have a whisky you might as well not have it and save a bit of money.

ANNE: Mr Positive! Just give me some bloody whisky.

MERVYN: *(going to the drinks table)* Are you mad with desire for it, is your tongue hanging out? Is it like the first time?

ANNE: Mervyn, you're getting boring.

MERVYN: Right. *(He pours whisky for himself and Anne)*

ANNE: As for the mediocrity of the product, that's *not* of my choosing.

MERVYN: What's that you say?

ANNE: Nothing. And do you really need any
more?

MERVYN: If I don't need it I want it. And if I don't
want it I need it. Anne's afraid I'm turning into an
alcoholic.

ANNE: Don't be ridiculous.

MERVYN: You mean you're not? I've been relying
on you to do the worrying for me. I have to do
everything myself. This calls for a drink. *(He
hands Anne her whisky)*

HELEN: I was a secret drinker. In the States. The
country's full of them.

MERVYN: *(laughing)* I was a Secret Drinker!
(sitting) What was your tipple?

HELEN: Gin. I started fortifying myself in the
afternoon, and then I found I was taking the
bottle to bed with me.

ANNE: In the afternoon?

HELEN: We had a TV at the foot of the bed. I'd lie
there through the afternoon watching the soap-
opera, all those empty confrontations. I used to
imagine the TV set was a kind of vivarium, full of
unhappy people, crawling over one another,
forced to go on and on, in spite of themselves,
for ever. Then I'd start to cry with the gin, and it
was as if I were in there too, crawling over bodies
in that glass tank; and then, if I was lucky, it was
all suddenly terribly funny, the meaninglessness of
it. Oh, the relief of that. Then I'd sleep. David
used to come home hoping for sympathy and a hot
supper, and find me in bed, blotto.

DAVID: One day I went downstairs. I had a small
hand-gun. I brought it up, and stood there for —
I don't know how long . . .

Pause

MERVYN: Well, enough chit-chat. Let's get down

to the nitty-gritty. David, tell me about the
therapy.

DAVID: What do you want to know?

MERVYN: Everything, Father, I want to know
everything! It really works, does it?

DAVID: It has for us.

MERVYN: Yes, I can believe that. You've both
changed, you know.

DAVID: I know.

MERVYN: You used to be very busy people, always
busying yourselves. Now there's a kind of tran-
quillity — no, that's wrong, a calm, a stillness at
the centre there. You've stopped smoking, you're
not drinking. Your voices are lower, I'm
convinced of it. And you had a trick with your leg,
you used to continually twitch your leg muscle.

DAVID: Did I?

HELEN: That's right, I'd forgotten.

MERVYN: You've both stopped twitching, that's
what it is. I was reading that people who've been
through the therapy sometimes find it quite a
strain having to deal with ordinary neurotics like
us. Is that true? It's all right, David, I can quite
believe it. People twitch all the time, even I notice
it sometimes and I'm a great twitcher. We twitch
cigarettes, we twitch drinks, we twitch conversation, we twitch each other and call it making
love . . . Well, it's all twitching, I suppose,
according to theory, the whole of adult behaviour,
a twitching away from the hurt of the childhood
trauma. And there you sit, the two of you, twitch-
less and apparently — I have to say it —
contented. I read the book, by the way. Twice.

DAVID: How did you find it?

MERVYN: Very disturbing.

DAVID: Disturbing, why?

MERVYN: The implications of it. It's difficult to
explain, I haven't thought it through properly,
there's something . . . What are *you* staring at?

ANNE: You didn't tell me *you* found it disturbing.

MERVYN: Well, I did. *(To David)* Anyway, tell me all about it. You don't mind, do you? Anne thought you might be embarrassed.

DAVID: Not at all.

MERVYN: You can leave out the grisly details.

DAVID: Anything you want to know.

HELEN: He likes talking about it.

MERVYN: Good. It'll be a treat for you. Was it the book put you on to it?

DAVID: Yes; one of those lucky chances. I picked it up in a book store. I was at my lowest, suicidal really — if I could have been positive. You know I had a breakdown.

MERVYN: You told me.

DAVID: I started to read it in the shop. It blew my mind. I thought, that's it, that's the way out, that's for me. Perhaps I'd have taken anything; it happened to be that, thank God. When I got home I realized I'd forgotten to pay for it.

MERVYN: And then you persuaded Helen.

HELEN: I made my own decision, Mervyn

MERVYN: Yes, of course.

DAVID: It was the simplicity of it got us; the simple logic of it. You know?

MERVYN: I know exactly what you mean.

HELEN: We managed to scrape the money together. We're still paying it off as a matter of fact.

MERVYN: With what you're saving on drinks and smokes.

DAVID: Exactly.

MERVYN: A good business proposition. You'll soon be making a profit. Where do I sign?

HELEN: It's not something to be laughed at.

MERVYN: No.

DAVID: Have you read it, Anne?

ANNE: No.

MERVYN: What? I saw you at it.

ANNE: Well, I didn't get far.

DAVID: Why not?

ANNE: At my time of life, David, it's not easy reading a book saying how simple and pleasant everything could have been.

DAVID: It still could — there's still time.

ANNE: Hm . . .

DAVID: I think everyone should read it.

MERVYN: Come, now, you don't mean should.

DAVID: No, right, I don't believe in "should". But I do think it's terribly important.

MERVYN: Why?

DAVID: Don't you think so?

MERVYN: I'm asking why *you* think it's important that everyone should read it. After all, you've had your therapy, you're home and dry.

DAVID: I still have to live in the world. It puts on a front, you know, a mask. After the therapy you see past that. You look at a smiling face and see the muscles holding the smile in place. You see through the eyes to the anger and resentment and fear. People are hanging on for dear life, and smiling. We're in extremity, Mervyn. We really are. I can imagine a future civilization looking back on this one, sifting through the evidence, if we leave any, and saying: My God, how did they survive? How could they bear to live like that?

MERVYN: Yes, I can imagine that. And you think you've found the answer.

DAVID: Yes, I do.

MERVYN: Good-bye, unhappiness.

DAVID: Good-bye, happiness. It's just as unreal, just as much part of the illness.

ANNE: Unreal? Happiness? Haven't you been happy ever?

DAVID: I've been neurotic. I've fooled myself.

ANNE: And now you don't. Congratulations.

DAVID: Sorry, do I sound patronizing?

ANNE: Yes.

DAVID: I don't mean to be.

HELEN: I think what David means . . .

ANNE: Let David say what he means. I have for one or two moments in my life thought, felt, I was happy, David. A few fleeting moments in the whole long stretch of it. No more than a handful of tiny diamonds — well, all right, sequins — stitched into a — a utility blanket. But at least I could say to myself later: there were these; they were real — sequins. There do exist, somewhere, sequins. Now you're saying they weren't real at all, just a neurotic fantasy. Well, and if they were, what's wrong with that, if it relieves the monotony? Why shouldn't we fool ourselves?

Slight pause.

DAVID: No reason, I suppose.

ANNE: Now you're humouring me.

DAVID: All right. The false is always wrong. The truth is always right. Happiness is a feeling of transcendence, of going beyond oneself, getting outside oneself.

ANNE: And that's wrong?

DAVID: It's false. There is no outside. There's my body, and the environment which is an extension of my body. That's all we have to enjoy, because that's all there is: our bodies, in our environment, now.

MERVYN: David, you're not suggesting an orgy?

DAVID: We are what we are: this, here. That has to be enough. There's nothing else. Nothing to reach out for. I do enjoy myself. More than ever before. I can feel myself living; now; here. I don't have to be happy.

MERVYN: And if that's not enough?

DAVID: If living in your own body isn't enough, that's the neurosis.

MERVYN: Full circle.

DAVID: The search after happiness — or perfection, or ideals, or anything else that seems to come from outside the world we live in — is to real life as pornography is to real sex.

MERVYN: I like that.

DAVID: What's so difficult? Look, I am a — an organism. I live in a physical world that supports me as I help support it. I live in space and time, in this space and in the present. Not somewhere else, or in some other time, or in some other world of spiritual values. I'm here, now.

MERVYN: Yes — yes . . .

HELEN: I think you've covered it now, David.

ANNE: And your mind, what about that?

DAVID: What about it?

ANNE: Oh, David, for God's sake . . .

DAVID: My mind isn't something else. It's not a traveller from outer space come to take possession of my body.

ANNE: I'm not saying it is . . .

DAVID: It's part of my body; or a quality of it, or a function of it. It's part of my sensory apparatus. It makes me aware of myself, aware of my surroundings, it allows me to communicate with my environment, recognize it and touch it. That's what I need it for and that's what it is. It does its job very well.

ANNE: So it's just a bit of the machinery.

DAVID: For living with. What more do you want?

ANNE: I don't know. Nothing: I suppose I agree with you. So why do I find your attitude so depressing?

MERVYN: Because you're neurotic, darling. Join the club.

ANNE: I wasn't asking you.

MERVYN: It's no good asking him, he's too kind to say.

DAVID: If the world your body lives in isn't enough, that's a neurosis, I've already said so. It just happens to be an almost universal neurosis, so it's assumed to be normal.

HELEN: Everyone's crazy except us . . .

DAVID: The world is crazy, that's generally accepted. All I'm saying is there's a way out of it.

MERVYN: The therapy.

DAVID: Yes. The therapy. I know it sounds simplistic; but there it is.

MERVYN: I agree with you.

DAVID: That it's simplistic?

MERVYN: That it's a way out.

DAVID: You do?

MERVYN: Don't look so surprised.

DAVID: So what are we arguing about?

MERVYN: I'm not arguing. I've drunk too much to argue.

ANNE: *In vino*, at last, *veritas*.

MERVYN: Yes, darling, if you can call this vino.

DAVID: Everyone wants to escape from the reality of just living. They want outside referees to tell them how they're getting on. They want value, they want meaning. That's what you're really asking for, isn't it? Meaning.

ANNE: Who, me? Yes, I suppose I am. Is that wrong?

DAVID: Misguided.

ANNE: There's no meaning.

DAVID: You want a yes or no.

ANNE: Yes, I do if you don't mind.

DAVID: Suppose the whole concept of meaning is meaningless? Suppose your question is unreal? We're sitting here talking; does it have meaning? Is there meaning in eating an ice cream? Or making love?

Slight pause

MERVYN: Yes and no, in that order.
DAVID: Neither yes nor no. Living is the meaning.
The meaning is living. Do you see? As soon as you
come back into your own body, into your own
experience, meaning stops having meaning.
There's no separation between what we do and
what it's for. There's only what we do. There isn't
another world behind this one giving it values.
There's one world, and this is it, and that's its
value. There's only living.
MERVYN: You're a bit of an existentialist, aren't
you?
DAVID: I'm *not* an existentialist. I'm not an ist.
I'm just living.

Slight pause

ANNE: And then dying.

The telephone rings. Mervyn goes to take it

DAVID: And then dying. Stopping living. Why
worry about that?
MERVYN: Hallo? . . . Who? . . . Sorry, you've got
the wrong number. *(He puts the receiver down)*
DAVID: If you're living in the present you don't
have to worry; and when you stop living you still
don't have to worry.

Pause

ANNE: I don't know whether that's very deep or
very shallow.
MERVYN: Wrong. Neither. You've fallen into the
same trap again, the yes or no trap. It's neither
deep nor shallow. It's not even superficially deep

or profoundly shallow. It's just a fact of his life.
It's the way he lives. It's therefore true. It's no
good, you can't fault it. What about you, Helen?
You're staying very quiet. What are your thoughts
on life, and death, and meaning, and eating ice
cream, and — what was the other thing? What do
you think about it all, behind those eyes I used to
find so — enigmatic?
ANNE: Behave, darling.
HELEN: I don't want to talk about it.
MERVYN: Why not?
HELEN: And I don't want to talk about why I
don't want to talk about it.
MERVYN: Fair enough. *(Pause)* Likewise morality.

Slight pause

ANNE: What the hell do you mean, likewise
morality? No, don't tell me. I don't think I want
to talk about any of this any more. Ever. I don't
think it *ever* does *any*body *any* good.
MERVYN: As meaning, likewise morality. An
abstraction, a mystical spin-off from reality, part
of that never-never land constructed, in its
imagination, by a neurotic culture which can't
bear the thought of nothing but the here and now
because, being neurotic, it doesn't enjoy it; and
which can't take responsibility for its own actions
because, being neurotic, it's rather vicious. How's
that for a summing-up? So, David, in your new-
won freedom, you never have to tell yourself you
shouldn't do something you want to do — I
suppose. Do you?
DAVID: I don't like hurting people, Mervyn. And I
want to help my society . . .
MERVYN: I'm not asking that, answer the
question.
DAVID: Then you're right. Given what I've just
said . . .

MERVYN: That a mentally healthy individual is of necessity moral.

DAVID: If you like. Healthy people don't want to hurt each other. Why should they? They gain nothing.

MERVYN: All right, given that.

DAVID: Given that, I don't have to think in terms of "should". It becomes a matter of advisability. One makes one's own decisions. I wouldn't put my hand into the fire, for instance, if you bet me a hundred pounds, not because that would be avarice and therefore a sin, but because I'd prefer not to.

MERVYN: A hundred thousand.

DAVID: For how long?

MERVYN: Erm — two minutes.

DAVID: I'll make that decision when I come to it.

MERVYN: All right, what about . . .? What if you were told, if you don't put your hand in the fire for — ten minutes, Helen there will be slowly — tortured to death; pincers, wires . . .

ANNE: Mervyn, darling!

DAVID: I imagine I'd do it. At least, I'd want to be able to.

MERVYN: Why?

DAVID: Because I'd rather have Helen than my hand.

MERVYN: That's good. What if . . .?

ANNE: Mervyn, do you mind!

MERVYN: Shush, this is a serious discussion. What if there was an absolute choice between you being tortured to death, and Helen being tortured to death?

DAVID: It's hypothetical. I can't say what decision I'd make.

MERVYN: What decision would you want to make?

DAVID: Mervyn, you don't understand. It's not a matter of wanting to make a particular decision,

only of making it as the need arises. I hope the
need for that decision never will arise. All right?

MERVYN: Yes . . .

ANNE: Right, can we get off that now?

The telephone rings. Mervyn takes it

MERVYN: Hallo . . . No, I'm afraid I'm still the
person who wasn't last time. Do you think you
could try the operator? . . . Not at all. *(He puts the
receiver down)* Now — David. What if . . .?

ANNE: Darling, I may get rather angry if you keep
on about this.

MERVYN: It's all right, the torture sessions's over:
that was a red herring, I see that now. David —
let's get it straight. There is only the body: no
outside references, no God, no moral imperatives,
no abstract values, these are all neurotic fantasies.
The healthy person lives in a state of benevolent
egoism, is that fair?

DAVID: Yes, given that . . .

MERVYN: Yes, yes, given that as a natural
consequence of his health he respects his fellows,
likes to give and receive love and doesn't want to
hurt anyone. O.K.?

DAVID: Yes . . .

MERVYN: His morality, in other words, comes out
of his own body as a natural expression of his love
and enjoyment of the life which is the only thing
he has. Right?

DAVID: That's very good.

MERVYN: I think so. Now: I'll try not to make it
hypothetical. Not: "What if you had to choose
between you dying and Helen dying?" —

ANNE: Oh God, Mervyn!

MERVYN: But: "Given a man in your happy
situation who's had this therapy, who's been
cured of his neuroses; and who has to choose

between his own death and his wife's; as it might
be, on an overloaded life-raft or a — Siberian
sleigh with the wolves drawing closer — which do
you think, in your good judgement, he would be
more likely to choose?''

Pause

DAVID: You'd make a good chess-player, Mervyn.
MERVYN: This isn't chess. It's a matter of life and
death. Look. *(He takes out a flick-knife and opens
it)* Confiscated yesterday; sharp as a razor. *(He
stands over David)* Now, make your choice. Your
or her, David. You or her.

Pause.

DAVID: All right. You win.
MERVYN: David, you're treating it like a game. It
isn't a game. It's bloody serious, don't you see?
Come on, she's asleep, you can say.
ANNE: Don't get unpleasant, darling . . .
MERVYN: Let me explain the state of play. White
King there has the choice of sacrificing his Queen
or being knocked off the board, in which case the
game is at an end. What is he to do in one move?
It's quite obvious. Why do you hesitate? You're
not that bad a chess-player. The game is all there
is, David; you can't get another life, but you can
always get another Queen. Don't tell me you
wouldn't want to live without her. After all, if
she died you wouldn't then kill yourself, would
you?
ANNE: Mervyn, that's enough!

Pause

DAVID: I think he made a very fair point.

ANNE: Yes, David, but I think we've had enough about it now.

MERVYN: I haven't. Have you, David?

DAVID: I don't mind.

ANNE: I mind, do you mind? I find this conversation rather upsetting. It's quite ridiculous, but I do.

MERVYN: That's because you're neurotic.

ANNE: Oh, shut up.

MERVYN: More Scotch?

ANNE: Yes.

MERVYN: There's nothing to it really. *(He refills the glass)* For the mentally healthy individual, cured of the pains of his childhood and thus balanced, non-belligerent and content to live life in the present, God is dead and there is no meaning.

DAVID: God was never alive and meaning is unnecessary.

MERVYN: Only watch out if you ever find yourself sharing a life-raft made for one with this nice sane guy: because he might just shove you out

DAVID: And in a spirit of self-sacrifice you might just let him.

Slight pause

MERVYN: Exactly.

Slight pause

HELEN: You are a cheat, Mervyn.

MERVYN: I thought you were asleep.

HELEN: I was listening. What a destructive cheat you are. With your logic.

MERVYN: How? Tell me.

HELEN: Oh, the usual way. Like anyone with a gift for words. It's all in the abstract for you, all in the

head. You bring things into existence by giving
them names, then you argue the toss about them.
And win, of course. You play with words. You're
a great player with words. And you're so good at
it, you almost convince us you're talking about
something real. That's where you cheat. Words
are not things, Mervyn, not actions, not feelings.
They're just noises you make in your head.
MERVYN: Words are all we have, Helen.
HELEN: Not true.
MERVYN: To think with.
HELEN: Thinking isn't everything. Have you ever
wondered how it is that when it comes to
something as complex and problematical as
bringing children into existence, women don't
usually philosophize about it, they just do it? But
my God, Mervyn, if you had the job . . .
MERVYN: I don't understand what you're saying.
HELEN: No, I don't suppose you do. It's too
simple for you, you can't do anything with it.
You've been making fun of what we've done . . .
MERVYN: That's not true!
HELEN: You seem to think we've locked ourselves
inside some sort of — tin castle, cut ourselves off,
made ourselves safe. And round and round you
go, because you feel you've been left out, looking
for some chink, some flaw; some crack you can
stick your stick of logical dynamite in. And blow
it sky-high, and us with it. There's no castle. You
imagine it. We're as vulnerable as you are. All
we've done is make ourselves a little more sane, a
little more comfortable, a little more able to cope.
There's nothing to blow up, Mervyn.
MERVYN: Honey, I wasn't trying to get at you . . .
HELEN: Yes, you were. Is that why you invited us?
Did you think we'd hooked on to some new false
faith that your logic could strip us of? You're
wasting your time. We're not a couple of

Jehovah's Witnesses. I suppose I used to believe in God, vaguely: I mean an ultimate balancing of the books, a final share-out where I'd get back what I'd lost and the others would pay for what they'd taken. I've lost that faith, the only one I ever had. I know I shall never get my own back. The losses are permanent. It's a painful lesson to have to learn; but I've done it, and now it doesn't matter. You can't take anything from us, Mervyn, because all we have is ourselves. Which we don't have to justify. We don't have to.

MERVYN: So much for the past?

HELEN: Yes.

MERVYN: It had no meaning outside itself. Whatever the waste and suffering, whatever the losses, it was in no way meant, or useful, or in a good cause, or redeemable — and whatsoever good things there were, whatever high and noble deeds, whatever pleasures, whatever loves, whatever raptures, that too is gone, and means nothing?

HELEN: What do you want it to mean?

MERVYN: I don't know. For Christ's sake, I don't know . . .

ANNE: Darling, do you know you're as pissed as a newt?

MERVYN: Yes, I had noticed. But thank you for reminding me. My trainer. It's the big fight tomorrow, she's worried about the weighing-in.

ANNE: What are you talking about?

HELEN: *(rising)* Actually I think it's time we were going.

MERVYN: What? You can't go yet!

HELEN: We can, Mervyn.

MERVYN: I know you can. I mean I don't want you to.

DAVID: It's just the drive. *(He rises)*

MERVYN: What's just the drive?

ANNE: Darling, if they want to go . . .

MERVYN: I don't give a shit if they want to go. I
want them to stay and I want to be selfish. Is that
all right?

ANNE: Oh dear, oh dear . . .

MERVYN: You haven't got baby-sitters, have you?
And you're certainly not worried about the breath
test.

DAVID: That's true.

MERVYN: It's Sunday tomorrow. You don't have
to go to Church. You're a well-integrated couple,
you can put up with us for a bit longer. Come on,
stay another ten minutes for old times' sake for
Christ sake. My friends, my old friends, my
loves . . .

Mervyn hugs David, then Helen

ANNE: Blackmail. Sheer moral bloody blackmail.

MERVYN: I know, I know, I'm everything base. Sit
down, sit down.

Helen and David sit.

ANNE: Can I make you a cup of tea?

HELEN: Not for me, thanks.

DAVID: I'm fine, thanks.

MERVYN: D'you see, they're fine, they're always
fine, these two.

ANNE: It's very interesting, Mervyn, that as soon
as I tell you you're pissed you start playing it.

MERVYN: Oh, God, do I even act being pissed? I
do, I do . . . Right, I shall now act being sober.
You see how easily we change our protective
colouring, we neurotics, well never mind that, I
must concentrate and distil, ten minutes I said,
yes? Because this therapy, David, or its implications, happen to be of vital importance to me, not
to say an obsession, put it down to the male

menopause if you like. The book was given me,
lent me, by . . . No, I'm going off the track.
Enough to say that something happened to the
lender, I rang you up, I began to read the book,
I rang you again to find you'd had the treatment,
I arranged to see you tonight when, I find,
something else is to happen to the lender — and I
began to wonder whether somebody was trying to
tell me something. Synchronicity, you know about
that? C. G. Jung was with a patient who was
telling of a vivid dream about a scarab: there was a
tapping on the window. A scarab-like beetle was
knocking to get in. So you see, Helen, I didn't
invite you *because of* the therapy, cause and effect
is not so simple . . . Where was I? Yes, you said it
blew your mind, David. Well, it blew mine too,
though not at first. I was sceptical, as you can
imagine, at my age one's lived through any
number of final solutions. When I found the book
talking about a *cure*, the psychiatrists' four-letter
word — a *cure* for neurosis, for the neurosis of
society, more or less guaranteed and all in a matter
of months, I admit I thought you must be in a really
bad way. It reminded me of the time you bought
those awful cylindrical things to stop you smoking
the easy way, do you remember? But I ploughed
on, and then read it again, and much to my
dismay it seemed to make sense.
DAVID: Why much to your dismay?
MERVYN: Because as you said, it makes everything
seem so bloody simple. You say that's what
attracted you to it: well, that's what put me off.
We're very different, you see, you and I, I mean
we always were different. I suppose it's the
difference between the businessman and the
teacher: you have to do it, I just have to talk about
it. So it didn't seem right, I know what you're
going to say.

DAVID: What?

MERVYN: Looking for difficulty is part of the neurosis. Right?

DAVID: I think there's an element of that.

MERVYN: After all, if life is so simple what excuse do we have for making such a cock-up of it? So we construct our edifices to justify our incompetence — My God, the sheer volume of psychiatric shit the world carries on its shoulders, and all invented in less than a century. What a strange metaphor, shit on the shoulders.

ANNE: Bird shit?

MERVYN: Thank you, darling. The droppings of the theoretical high-flyers, the great auks of psychoanalysis.

ANNE: Great auks couldn't fly, darling. They only had rudimentary wings.

MERVYN: Exactly! They convinced us, though, didn't they? Flapping about across the intellectual tundra, rudimentary wings going like ninepence. My God, we cried, look at them go! Look at them fly! Freud, Jung, Reich, and all their brood; Laing levitating in the lotus position. Only none of it bloody works; let's face it, it self-evidently doesn't bloody *work*. Not one of them dared talk about a cure, not until this one. He *cures*. And why not? There's obviously something wrong with us all, as you say, look at the world. If there's one thing all the great auks agree on, one chorus that recurs in all that twittering, it's that we carry about with us, one and all, an almost intolerable burden of hang-up. The shit on the other shoulder. There are those who say it's of the condition of man. I've never gone along with that, natural selection wouldn't allow it. Whatever it is, it ought to be possible to get rid of it; somewhere on earth by the law of averages there ought to be a sane person who can say: This is what is wrong

with you, you idiots; and this is how I propose to
put it right. And here it is in the book; the Messiah
has arrived at last: case histories and all. And the
words inscribed on the rock are these: Injuries
occur in childhood, shock the child can't cope
with. The pains are repressed and the result is a
fuck up. So don't humour the patient. Don't re-
inforce the repression. Don't play Freud's game.
There is no original sin, no built-in trauma, people
are really *nice*. Nastiness is removable. All you
have to do is help the patient dig up those nuggets
of hurt; make him feel them, make him accept the
pain, feel the pain, scream the pain out. And all
will be light and reason. And there are you two,
light and reason if I ever saw it. No, I'm not being
snide, I mean it. I remember you as you were:
your arrogance, David, your terror of losing out,
so endearing: and Helen, so funny, so bright, so
hysterical. I'll tell you the real difference. We
neurotics, we put on images, don't we, coats of
many colours. We play parts to protect ourselves
or entertain each other. We're the sympathetic
characters, of course, we make sure of that; our
excesses, our stupidities, our drunken ramblings,
people love them, everyone loves a show. Whereas
all you've got, as you say, is yourselves; no cover-
up, no entertaining gloss, no funny nose or
peacock-tail. All you can provide is reality, what
a yawn, the reality of yourselves; which starts on
the surface and goes all the way through, doesn't
it? So that when, as now, Helen sees through the
act I can't help putting on, her eyes fill with tears.
That's good, no barriers there, no false fronts,
just a living in the body in an environment which
happens at the moment to be not too nice. And I
look for something you've lost, you two, I admit
it, something I can use to write your therapy off;
and I can't, in reason, find it. More whisky,
darling? *(He pours himself some more)*

DAVID: I don't really understand you, Mervyn. If
you don't believe it, why . . .?
MERVYN: Of course I bloody believe it! For
Christ's sake, don't you understand what I'm
saying? I haven't been able to *not* believe it!
ANNE: Keep your voice down, darling.
MERVYN: What?
ANNE: You were shouting.
MERVYN: Darling, we don't have kids any more,
do you remember, we sent them off to make their
own mistakes? There's no Mrs — what-was-her-
name to bang on the wall. We're a settled middle-
class rate-paying couple approaching the evening
of our lives and if I can still find something in the
world which seems to be of importance to me, for
Christ's sake allow me to raise my voice a little.
(Pause.) Oh God, this is all going wrong . . .

Pause

HELEN: Let's go, David.
DAVID: Yes, in a minute. The trouble is, Mervyn,
I don't exactly know what your problem is.
ANNE: I do. It's envy, isn't it?

Mervyn looks at Anne

It is for me. When I heard you'd had some sort of
therapy, which had worked, I felt a little pang of
resentment. It's awful, isn't it? So, I thought,
they're out of it; they've escaped. I'm left. It made
me feel rather inadequate, rather rejected.
DAVID: It's not like that . . .
ANNE: It is. You know that expression, "Coming
to terms with things?" You read an article about
one of the various problems, how to cope when
the kids leave home, how to cope with a broken
marriage, how to cope with middle-age; you skip

to the end for the answer, since you know the
problem already, and there it is: Come to terms
with it. I don't think I've ever come to terms with
anything in my life. I don't know what it means.
They're all still there, the old battlefields, silted
over but still there, the old resentments, just below
the surface like rusty bayonets. Nothing's
finished. I suppose we'll take it to the grave with
us, the unpaid scores, the regrets, the bitterness of
all those defeats; with no idea what the fighting
was all about. I shan't make a good death. *(To
Mervyn)* Neither will you. We'll go down cursing
. . . And when I step on to the further shore the
first thing I shall do is ask for my money back. Of
course we're envious. What do you expect? What
did you expect? Why did you come? You must
have known.

DAVID: We were asked, Anne.

ANNE: Of course, you were always good at coming
when you were asked, weren't you?

MERVYN: Naughty darling . . .

ANNE: Why, now? Lest old acquaintance be
forgot, surely not; it's all the same whether they're
forgot or not, isn't it? The past is not your bag, is
it? Concreted over, your battlefields; the bad
times, and the good times . . .

DAVID: It wasn't easy for us, you know.

ANNE: I don't suppose it was. I'm sure it was very
unpleasant for you, having to relive all that old
stuff. It's easy now, though, isn't it?

DAVID: I don't think easy is the right word.

ANNE: What is the right word? *(To Mervyn)*
You're good at words, darling, what's the right
word?

DAVID: You don't forget things. You have to re-
remember; it all comes back. It's a very painful
process. *(Slight pause)* I haven't rejected the past.
I still think about it. It still affects me. Only I'm
not bound to it any more, I've . . .

ANNE: Come to terms with it. Bully for you,
David. Before you pass out, Mervyn, would you
mind handing over the Scotch?

*Mervyn pours her a drink, watches her, then looks
at them*

MERVYN: Aren't we pussyfooting? Oh aren't we
playing it safe though?
ANNE: Now, darling . . .
MERVYN: Don't now darling me, darling. If there's
something you want to say why don't you say it
for Christ's sake in good plain English? *(He looks
at the other two)* We all fucked each other, don't
you remember?
ANNE: Dar-*ling*.
MERVYN: All right, I'm sorry, that's putting it too
crudely. After all, what's a bit of fucking between
friends? We — *knew* one another is what I mean.
We made ourselves naked to each other, we were
vulnerable together, we gave ourselves to each
other; we clung to one another, in desperation and
in delight and in defeat. We gave ourselves away.
And what the wife's asking, David, if I may
interpret, is: do you remember that dead old
thing, now that you're cured? Do you ever visit
the grave? Is there a stone, or a bit of wood,
marking a spot in the wilderness? And if there is,
what have you inscribed on it for passing travellers
to read? "Here lie the remains of a neurotic
attachment"? What about you, Helen? What
have you done with it all? Was it a cremation, an
oven job? Did you have any trouble pulverizing
the last recognizable bits? If I touched you now,
there, or there, would you give a slight shiver as if
there were donkeys on your grave? Would a two-
minute silence help?

Pause

ANNE: Enough, Mervyn . . .

DAVID: You completely misunderstand. It's not *like* that. It's not a lobotomy we've had. Nothing's been cut out.

MERVYN: Has it not? Where is it, then, all that experience? Show us your wounds. Are you loath to, like Coriolanus, or haven't you got any? We have; we'll show them to anyone, won't we, darling, we've no pride. We're a couple of old campaigners, with a lifetime of scars to prove it. We'll talk of old battles, restage them if you like, won't we, darling, my old comrade? Going over the top together, lying in the mud together, staunching each other's blood. We've seen service, and the war still goes on, the scars still form on scars. But where are you marked, you two, where?

Pause

HELEN: David, I'd like to go now. *(She starts to rise)*

MERVYN: Oh, do sit down, Helen, do. Please, please, please . . . Because I haven't said it yet, I haven't got around to saying it yet. Give me a minute. The fellow who lent me the book, David, he was a strange, unlikeable lad. He was so — disconnected he didn't really believe in the physical world; he treated it like some kind of conjuring trick; as if he was waiting to see how it was done. Even his own body he carried around as if he were looking for its owner to give it back. Like a Martian in bad disguise. Though even a Martian would have accepted gravity; *he* didn't. I caught him once solemnly dropping his pen on to the desk like this; picking it up and letting it go. I asked him what he was doing, and he looked up in

surprise, as if he were amazed there were beings in
the world who thought they could communicate
with him. "Testing gravity," he said. In the
middle of a discussion of the sacred and profane
love poems of John Donne, Simpson was testing
gravity. I asked if it worked, keeping my temper.
"Usually," he said. But he was no idiot; he was
the brightest one there — including me, I think.
He had two obsessions, poetry and his motor-
bike. He'd sit, picking his spots, while we analysed
Shelley, then off he'd roar. He was a disruptive
influence, I hated him. I'd be talking about style
and he'd break in: "Is it better to write love
poetry, read love poetry, talk about love poetry,
or make love?" With his sickly smile. You
arrogant sod, I thought, you try teaching Eng. Lit.
to a bunch of sexually repressed louts. I didn't
need him to call into question what we were all
doing there. Stuck in a classroom with the sun
shining outside, discussing words, discussing
second-hand experiences, not even the experiences, too near the knuckle that, but the *style*.
At least you market paper, what do I market?
Then he took to hanging around after the others
had gone, with his worried smell. You know that
smell? Something in the sweat, nature's warning
to potential mates: Do not use. He showed me
some stuff he'd written; it wasn't up to much. I
didn't know what he wanted of me. Then one day
he brought me the book, said he'd like to know
what I thought of it. I had a quick look, thought,
Christ, I'm not getting into that, not with him. He
kept asking if I'd read it, it was obviously
important to him: I said no, not yet, I haven't
had time. It wasn't till afterwards I read it
properly. *Then* I saw what he'd wanted: to be
cured of being Simpson, no less. What a carrot to
dangle in front of the poor bugger. He probably

did what I did: searched for a flaw in the
argument, for a way to reject the feeling that it
made sense, felt right, seemed to work, that it
might actually be a true account, with all the
bullshit removed, of what we are really about.
DAVID: Why not?
MERVYN: Why not, why not embrace the possibility of this simple, sane future? Because,
David, the bullshit, and Simpson would have
realized this, includes not only the sort of neurotic
clinging to past hurts that we've been indulging in
this evening, but a little thing called art; that most
refined expression of neurosis. If the body is all
there is, there's no room for art, no room for
mystery, no room for the poetic experience.
Simpson wouldn't have known a thing about the
sort of antics we got up to, except from dirty
books; but he knew about the poetic experience.
For poor old Simpson the poetic experience was
the only decent thing he had in life; apart from his
motor-bike. So he had a problem, you see, and
whether it was a practical or theoretical one
doesn't really matter. He saw the dilemma: and he
couldn't solve it. So he took a third way out.
Made a botch of it of course, and got stuck
halfway. And his lungs are still pumping and his
heart is still beating, unless that bitch of a nurse
has let me down, by courtesy of twentieth-century
technology.

*The telephone rings twice. Before anyone can get
up to it, it stops*

DAVID: You're talking rubbish, Mervyn. You
know it. It's a false problem. Do you think we've
turned into a couple of Philistines? There's still
poetry, why not? There's still music. I can still be
made glad by it, or sad by it . . .

MERVYN: Glad and sad! You're talking about
verse; the entertainment of the senses, the
exchange of pleasing sensations. That's not art,
that's the bloody coach-trade. I'm talking about
that thing behind the words, behind the music, the
quality you can't teach, can't criticize, can't pin
down. That's what your therapy will cure us of, if
it's true — and it may be; the intimations in it, the
hints at something behind the fucking —
practicality we're stuck in, the hints that catch
your heart and fill you with wonder. What ode
would you write on a Grecian urn, David? "Heard
melodies are sweet, but those unheard are
sweeter?" Not on your life, "Beauty is truth,
truth beauty?" Rubbish. Keats was a bloody
neurotic. We'd gut him of that neurotic nonsense,
gut him of that sense of loss which is what art is all
about, that sense of something missed, something
just out of reach, something of wonder and value
and delight that lives on the edge of experience.
Beethoven and Bach could still churn out tunes to
make you glad and sad, though never to make
your heart suddenly stop. Chekhov would write
nice light comedies and Michelangelo would be a
happily married heterosexual, why carve bodies
out of chunks of rock when you can content
yourself with real ones? And so for the rest of
them . . . So what should I have said to Simpson,
if I'd let him ask his question? Get yourself
straightened out, lad? Or should I have said:
Look, Simpson, you're a spotty hung-up apology
for a human being and I appreciate your distress:
but you'll just have to put up with it, because
that's the way someone wants you. Accept
yourself, even if no-one else does. *Nil carborundum*:
don't let the bastards grind you down, or they'll
grind your balls off. Don't let them rip out your
faith.

ANNE: Are you going to sit down, darling, before you fall down?

MERVYN: That's the wife . . .

HELEN: So it boils down to a matter of faith?

MERVYN: What does, my love?

HELEN: Your argument. Leaving aside the rhetoric. You think we've lost something, which you still have: but you can't define it. You find your values threatened, but you don't know quite what they are or why they're valuable, or what their purpose is. So you talk about faith.

DAVID: It puts you in questionable company. I always thought you were a rationalist.

MERVYN: So did I. There you are, I haven't a leg to stand on; my bluff's been called by your bloody therapy. Perhaps the world's finding its reason at last and I don't like it. The old neurosis will be toppled like the statue of a deposed tyrant, and there'll be dancing in the market place. Down with the old order. No more searching through the dead past looking for value; no more chasing after meaning, no more attempting the impossible, no more seeking the delight not of this world and no more disappointment that it seems always just out of reach; no more struggle, no more torment, never again need anyone die for a cause, or a friend, or give himself to a stranger, for no good reason. There'll come a voluntary burning of pernicious books by reasonable people, the end of the old neurosis. And the surviving nuts will stand warming their hands at it, watching the smoke rise, with irrational tears running down their cheeks, and nothing left to sustain them but a memory of a dead faith, and no way to express their feelings but an empty rhetoric . . .

Pause

ANNE: Are you going to let them go now, darling?
HELEN: It's a sad image you have of yourself.
MERVYN: I suppose it is.
HELEN: You cling to that, don't you? The sadness
of it. The sadness of loss. Loss of love, loss of the
past, loss of value, loss of meaning. You're a
romantic, you're in love with loss. You hoard it
like a miser, count it over. You worry about the
loss of art, and what does art mean to you? A
sense of loss. You invite us here, but not to see us;
it's the past you're looking for. You can't switch it
off, can you? If *you* were in charge of that
machine, keeping that poor boy in limbo, you'd
leave him there, wouldn't you? You couldn't
bring yourself to decently end him; mourn for him
a little, and then forget him decently. You need
him there, to use him. His loss is your possession.
As for what I've done with what happened
between us, Mervyn, I've done nothing with it.
It's not there to do anything with. I remember it; I
remember the intensity of it, the pain and delight.
But that's not what you want. You want the
comfort back; the comfort of a love — it was a
kind of love — that you knew couldn't last. Its
loss was built in. You wanted that. And I
remember us clinging together for comfort; even
your voice, once, somewhere: Comfort me,
Helen; comfort me. We did what we could for
each other, took what we could from each other, it
was necessary. But not any more; I don't need it,
and I can't comfort you. I haven't written it off.
When it happened, it meant what it meant. Now,
it means nothing.

*Pause. Mervyn gets himself another drink. The
telephone rings. It goes on ringing, as Anne waits
for Mervyn to answer it. Instead, he starts talking
over it; Anne answers it*

MERVYN: Here's a thought. What if the quality that sets man above the rest of the animals, if that's where we want to be, is not the ability to make fire or words or weapons but the blessed gift of irrationality, the God-given capacity to be wilfully illogical, to be — *absurd*.

DAVID: Oh, Mervyn . . .

MERVYN: Don't laugh. It may be true. What's more irrational than the random mutation, and where would we be without that? What if my neurosis is all I have as a human being, to keep me moving?

DAVID: You really do cheat, You can't win with logic so you say we all need to be illogical. You are a charlatan.

MERVYN: It's one way out.

DAVID: It won't do, Mervyn.

MERVYN: It'll do, for want of something better. *Nil carborundum*.

"Say not the struggle nought availeth,
    The labour and the wounds are vain . . ."

Anne puts the receiver down. Mervyn looks across at her. She says nothing. He turns back to the others

If the worst comes to the worst, I can always buy myself a motor-bike. Joking, darling, joking . . .

CURTAIN